GHOSTS AND LEGENDS OF WOOD COUNTY, OHIO

MELISSA R. DAVIES

Haunted America

Published by Haunted America
A division of The History Press
Charleston, SC
www.historypress.com

Unless otherwise noted, all images are courtesy of the author's collection.

First published 2023

Manufactured in the United States

ISBN 9781467152570

Library of Congress Control Number: 2023937198

Notice: The information in this book is true and complete to the best of our knowledge. It is offered without guarantee on the part of the authors or The History Press. The authors and The History Press disclaim all liability in connection with the use of this book.

Stay, illusion!
If thou hast any sound, or use a voice.
Speak to me.
—Hamlet, *act I, scene I, line 140.*
Horatio, on seeing the Ghost.

CONTENTS

PREFACE

My first personal experience with things that go bump in the night came unexpectedly, in the spring of 1996. One glorious sunny day, about a dozen college classmates and I tumbled out of two overpacked extended vans. Our feet landed on the grounds of Chowan College in Murfreesboro, North Carolina. Our journey took us over seven hundred miles from our home school in Ohio, Defiance College. The trip wasn't as long and tedious as it would be now. I'm forty-six today, and the idea of a long ride cramped with too many bodies in one vehicle holds no appeal. Back then, however, at nineteen, the whole thing was a joyous excursion into a big world I had just begun exploring.

After more than a few group sing-alongs to *Jagged Little Pill*, we finally arrived at our destination. Chowan College (now Chowan University) is a small institution of about one thousand students, similar to Defiance College. It was initially founded in 1848 as a four-year women's college. We had been sent to help complete light renovations on the third floor of the historic McDowell Columns Building. This 1852 Greek Revival stucco structure still stands and houses administrative offices for the president and provost and the financial aid office. Our goal was to help preserve this location listed in the National Register of Historic Places. One purpose of our trip was to complete acts of service that would benefit the institution and the surrounding community. I was a member of what was called the Service Leaders. We were awarded fellowships for the length of our time as students as long as we completed acts of community service meant to augment our learning. This required giving up free time, like spring break, for the sake of helping others.

Back then, McDowell Columns needed minor updates, which we managed with a little elbow grease. This included tasks like deep cleaning, painting and minor repairs. Given Chowan's tight budget, we offered our services to help cut costs. This allowed more resources to go toward the school's primary mission of education. For the duration of our weeklong stay, we slept in dorm rooms located on the third floor.

After hauling my luggage up the stairwell and stepping into the hallway, I remember a strange sensation coming over me. The atmosphere was charged with an energy that was in stark contrast to how it felt climbing the stairs. It was so noticeable, in fact, that I stopped in my tracks to take it in. As others whizzed by me, heading to their assigned rooms, I stared at the hazy glow of fluorescent lights hanging from the ceiling, wondering if that somehow accounted for what I was feeling.

After only a moment or two, I shrugged it off and started looking for the room I'd be sharing with a friend. It took longer to find it than it should have, being situated down a small, darkened hallway that branched off the main hall. The lights had burned out, a repair that was already included on our list of things to do for the week. Groping around in the darkness, I finally came to my room's door and opened it. I was greeted by daylight pouring through the windows inside. The sun was just about to set on that first evening. Dinner would soon be served, followed by a meeting to go over the agenda for the days ahead. Chowan staff encouraged us to ask any questions that came to mind.

I had a question about the eerie feeling the place was giving me but no idea how to ask it. Instead, I listened patiently to the staff's instructions. For a reason that will soon become clear, I specifically remembered the rule about quiet time. Quiet was expected after ten o'clock each night to allow us to fully rest up for the next day's work. Knowing our rowdy bunch, I doubted we could abide by it. I went to bed wondering when one of us would cave first.

The answer, it seemed, was two nights.

On the second night, I lay in bed staring at the ceiling, annoyed. Someone was running up and down our hallway, giggling. It was one thing for someone to have an impromptu party in their room. I expected that much. It was another thing to take the party into the hallway outside my door, again and again. I was exhausted from a day of painting and really wanted to rest for another day of the same. I envied my roommate's heavy sleeping. She didn't even stir at the noise. The racket dragged on and on.

When my patience ran out, I sprang to my feet and grasped the doorknob. When I heard the next set of footsteps approaching, I flung the door open to surprise and confront the pest.

The surprise was mine. What greeted me on opening the door was a darkened silence. It was as though opening the door was an off switch of sorts, like pressing the stop button on a CD player. No one was around. I stood there stunned, recalling the foreboding sensation I'd had on first coming to the floor. I then shut the door quickly and skittered to bed, pulling the covers tight around me. The silence remained for the rest of the night, but the confusion in my head was relentless. I didn't sleep a wink.

I didn't tell anyone of the experience, fearing ridicule and disbelief. I'll admit it was tricky keeping my cool on the nights that followed. Thankfully, they were quiet and uneventful. But one other issue did pop up in a peculiar way. One morning, I complained to my roommate about how long it took for my curling iron to heat up. I always left it on the dresser, making sure to unplug it each time I finished. A bright indicator light shone when it was plugged in, something I would have certainly noticed at bedtime had I left it plugged in. Despite this, the next day I awoke to a hot, plugged-in curling iron ready to go. No waiting. Only more confusion.

My roommate was still asleep when I discovered it.

When it came time for us to leave, we all gathered for a farewell meal. After sharing our experiences and exchanging goodbyes, the time came for packing up for the long trip home. As the others busied themselves, I gathered the courage to approach the Chowan staff member who had organized our stay. She was a kindly looking middle-aged woman; someone I thought might have the patience to hear me out. I told her the whole story: the odd feelings at the start and the unexplained events that followed.

Her first reaction was one of curiosity. As I continued, this shifted into confirmation, as though I was telling her about something she already knew. In hushed tones, she leaned forward and explained that claims of unusual experiences on this floor had been reported for a long time. Nothing bad or harmful had ever happened to those who experienced them. However, the college's official policy was not to speak of the phenomenon for fear of generating hype. They didn't want students to be afraid of the building. After all, the reason we went there was to support the building's continued use and preservation.

The woman finally said that a long time ago a young woman had died on the third floor under tragic circumstances. She was not at liberty to share details of the story.

Fast-forward more than a couple decades, and the echoes of that experience linger for me. It sparked a fascination with events I can't explain. That's why I created a podcast, *Ohio Folklore*, which delves into legendary stories across the state. Later, when I was asked to write a book specific to the legends of Wood County, I leapt at the chance. I'm so fortunate to share my passion with you, the reader. In these pages, we'll explore legendary stories from across the county, some you may have heard of, others you may not. Each of them will leave you pondering a bit more about the places you've driven by countless times. If reading this book achieves that much, I'll call it a success.

Is Wood County haunted? Sure, in the same way Ohio's other eighty-seven counties are haunted. Legendary stories are everywhere. Having researched these stories for years, I've come to an important conclusion. Often, when unusual happenings keep occurring in one spot, there's a reason for it. Scratching a bit under the surface, into the historical record, reveals an unresolved past, one worthy of the restless spirits working to make themselves known. So, let's consider what souls from Wood County's ancient and more recent past might have to tell us. Their lives hold lessons worth knowing in these tumultuous times.

Perhaps these spirits don't mean to scare us but to leave some parting wisdom. Let's learn what they have to say.

Acknowledgements

Among the best parts of writing this book about local lore are the locals I've come to know in the process. Over the course of my research, I've encountered folks who share my passion for strange and unexplained spiritual forces. I'd like to offer my deepest gratitude for their contributions. Without their support, the following stories would lack depth and personal meaning. I'd like to thank the following people, in no particular order:

Staff members at BGSU, who wish to remain anonymous, shared their stories of unexplained experiences on campus. These accounts provided a foundation for further research that later revealed a hero's sacrifice. Because of them, this story is once again remembered.

Reference archivists for the Center for Archival Collections at Bowling Green State University's Jerome Library provided invaluable records from historical *Bee Gee News* articles. Particular thanks goes to Sara Butler-Tongate for her efforts in connecting me with much-needed resources.

Amy Craft Ahrens, owner of the For Keeps gift shop at 144 South Main in Bowling Green, generously shared stories of resident ghost "Frank," who inhabits the second floor. Her passion for things we cannot explain is much appreciated.

George Strata, owner of Beckett's Burger Bar, and son Jake Strata provided a tour of their historic building at 163 South Main Street in Bowling Green. It appears that this trendy eatery isn't only popular with the living. This story's inclusion in the book is so valued.

Jodie Domer, with the Wood County Clerk of Courts, is owed a debt of gratitude. She dug into dusty, decades-old court case files. She took the time to help me get reacquainted with a microfiche machine. Without her, these stories would lack historical depth and credence.

I'd like to thank the volunteer guides at Fort Meigs provided by the Old Northwest Military History Association (https://onmha.org). Thanks for helping the past come alive so we can learn the lessons of those who once trod the ground beneath our feet.

Matt Erman, director of the movie *The Legend of Holcomb Road*, graciously shared his knowledge of the subject. His enthusiasm for this local folktale has helped cement its place in Wood County lore.

Brian Redmond, PhD, Curator and John Otis Hower Chair of Archaeology at the Cleveland Museum of Natural History, provided critical insights regarding the Indian Hills site. His devotion to the preservation of Ohio's Native heritage is deeply valued.

Dave Misko, investigator with the Paranormal Mysteries team, provided critical access to the Indian Hills Elementary School in Rossford. He graciously shared his time and investigative experiences. Without him, my knowledge of this structure would be surface level at best.

Brian Dreier-Morgan, another member of the Paranormal Mysteries team and of Lake Erie Paranormal, provided invaluable background information on the land surrounding Indian Hills Elementary School. As a man of Cherokee descent, his research into the ancient Native village and burial grounds was integral to this book. He helped deepen my understanding of the significance of this place in Wood County's history. While this land's future remains in doubt at the time of this writing, may its stories remain in our collective memories from this day forward.

Nancy Stonerock, a Rossford native, was ninety-one years old when I interviewed her for this book. I was introduced to her by her daughter, Laura Martin. In the late 1950s, Nancy was the den mother for her sons' Cub Scouts troop. Their hike into what was then called Crane's Woods sparked further curiosity into the history of the Indian Hills site. She graciously shared her experiences for inclusion in this book.

Don Collins and Kelly Scheufler of Fringe Paranormal Investigations provided critical background on South Main School at 437 South Main Street in Bowling Green. Their tireless efforts to preserve this historic structure have not gone unnoticed. Although the building is no longer open for investigations, the Fringe team continues its mission to "explain the unexplained." Their efforts in helping me achieve this very goal are greatly appreciated.

To my parents, Roger and Nora Luersman, I offer many thanks for their lifelong support of all my interests. It's such love that enables me to take on any passion that strikes my fancy. Thanks, Mom and Dad.

Last but not least, I owe a debt to Jeremy Davies, my husband and constant supporter. He abides my obsessions, like chasing ghost tales and fantastic stories. He helps in any way possible, with no hesitation. This work was made better by him.

WOOD COUNTY, A BRIEF HISTORY

Today, Wood County is most known for the city of Bowling Green, its county seat. This college town draws folks from all over the country for its National Tractor Pull Championships every August. The city is surrounded by endless rows of corn, wheat and soybeans among flattened fields that once composed the Great Black Swamp. Rural influences weigh heavily on its culture, seen easily in yearly celebrations of the Wood County Fair. And yet, Wood County's country roots aren't all it has to offer residents and visitors alike.

BG (as the locals call Bowling Green) has a public university of around twenty thousand students. Bowling Green State University (BGSU) is a research institution with stately academic buildings within the 1,300-acre campus. The university's influence is seen in events throughout the city, like educational programming and the arts and music scene downtown, not to mention frequent flybys of propeller-driven airplanes operated by aspiring student pilots.

While that summarizes what Wood County is about today, it's worth taking a deeper dive into just what led up to that reputation. Let's examine some of the more difficult, daring and macabre aspects of Wood County history.

Although the city of Bowling Green wouldn't be incorporated until 1901, settlers began arriving in the early 1800s. The county itself was founded in 1820. Pioneers who first set foot on Wood County soil found a wet, soppy mess infested with malaria-carrying mosquitoes. Before the land was drained, any task proved almost impossible in land that swallowed up wagon wheels and horses' hooves. Today, a vast network of drainage tile has eliminated the standing water that once permeated the land. The herculean effort to rid the swamp of its swampiness created some of the richest and most fertile farmland in this section of the country.

For those early settlers unlucky enough to contract malaria, the symptoms began with recurring fever every three to four days, followed by a tender, swollen spleen and, later, a yellowish complexion. The most unfortunate of those stricken went on to suffer kidney failure, seizures and coma. Many died in a godforsaken wilderness as helpless others looked on in pity.

Accounts from soldiers during the War of 1812 tell of marches through mud that reached their thighs. Frequent stops were needed to pull wagons and horses from the infernal muck. And when they finally set up camp, pitching tents to get a full night's rest, the water would inevitably seep in, inches deep, before the men woke the next morning. Worse than this were the ever-present mosquitoes, hungry for human blood. These nascent U.S. troops suffered more casualties to that damned insect than to the entirety of the King's army.

While Americans defended their land from a foreign invader for the first time, they also systematically attacked, invaded, murdered and forcibly removed Native peoples from this same land. Wood County's charter followed the Lower Maumee Treaty of 1817. This land was "purchased" from local tribes, including the Shawnee, Wyandot, Seneca, Ottawa, Potawatomi, Chippewa and Delaware. Facing no real choice but annihilation, these tribes had to accept terms of exile from lands inhabited by their ancestors for centuries. Slayings of countless Native peoples were left unchronicled in pioneer records.

The county was named in honor of Captain Eleazer Derby Wood, commanding officer of the Northwestern Army in 1812. He oversaw the construction of Fort Meigs, one of Wood County's most beloved historic sites. We'll learn more about this spirited place in the pages ahead.

Fast-forward more than a century, and infectious disease once again beleaguered Wood County residents. Local officials attempted to contain deadly outbreaks of Spanish flu and tuberculosis using a pestilence house. This structure, which still stands on the grounds of today's Wood County Museum, served to quarantine residents who suffered these dreaded, contagious diseases. (The Wood County Museum site was considered for a chapter in this book. Its director declined participation, citing a board policy against any media coverage of paranormal activity at the museum.)

The brief history included in this introduction can't possibly address all of what is notable about Wood County's past. The good news, however, is that such history is waiting to be discovered. With a little patience and effort in this day of information technology, the legends of our ancestors are knowable. They are written in historical newspapers, in court records and in tales passed down through the generations.

May we remember the lessons they bring.

1

MAN-IN-TAN

BGSU's FORGOTTEN GHOST

A hero is someone who understands the responsibility that comes with his freedom.
—*Bob Dylan*

No book recounting legendary stories from Wood County, Ohio, would be complete without a reference to the venerable institution known as Bowling Green State University.

Established in 1910, this public research university has seen more than its fair share of unique characters over the decades. It has a current enrollment of about twenty thousand. Students of all cultures and backgrounds have traversed its grounds, sauntered along its hallways and performed on its stages.

Two such performance spaces were once known as the Eva Marie Saint and Joe E. Brown Theaters. Both were housed in a section of University Hall recently demolished, in March 2016. University Hall itself still stands as a historic structure. It now houses offices, classrooms and student programs.

Even though these theaters were razed, something of the shadow of their influence remains. Their haunting reputation was well known during their life spans. One mischievous spirit was so active that she had a name: Alice. She was known for ghostly pranks like misplaced props, flickering lights and audio problems. To ward against this, stage managers invited her to the show before each opening night with a soliloquy that even Romeo would have admired. Then, one prime seat in the audience was roped off, saved for her viewing pleasure.

The official seal of Bowling Green State University outside University Hall. Legend has it that if sweethearts stand on the seal and kiss at midnight, they will soon be married.

University Hall at Bowling Green State University, 2022.

East lobby of University Hall, former hat room for former theaters once housed there.

The other resident ghost of these two former theaters is the subject matter of our story. Although he is not well known to current students and staff, his supposed existence has been chronicled in local newspapers for years. While the stages themselves have long been dismantled, the specific spot he allegedly haunts does remain today. The space that once served as the theaters' hat room is now a lobby area for one of University Hall's entrances.

When the theaters were in operation, audience members frequented this space, dropping off heavy clothing and hats so they could enjoy performances in comfort. With some regularity, male audience members developed a feeling of unease when approaching the reception window. Some fidgeted, sensing an electric feeling of unwelcome. Others rushed off to their seats with nervous energy. By contrast, women were known to report the opposite sensation. Many commented on a sense of warmth and protection surrounding them. Some lingered in the space, looking around and seeking the source of their unexpected reception.

Any given person's feelings are as spontaneous and unpredictable as the wind. But when such occurrences keep happening, specific to one's gender, the pattern became undeniable. What made the whole thing intriguing is the fact that each new experiencer knew nothing of the countless others who'd gone before them. The workers in the hat room first came to recognize these strange displays of emotions among their male and female customers.

In time, this peculiar collection of emotional reactions from unrelated theatergoers sparked a kind of folktale to explain it. The story went that in the 1940s, one prolific student-musician had been known to walk women home to their dormitories after each performance. Ever the gentleman, he took the protective role of an older brother, ensuring that his fellow female performers got home safely. As the story went, one night after a performance, our chivalrous student decided to stay at the theater for an impromptu party. This left one female performer to head to her room alone. A full load of classes awaited her the next day. Tragically, she never made it to those classes. It's said that she was sexually assaulted and murdered before making it to the dormitory's front entrance.

The folktale proclaims that the young man never forgave himself for allowing this poor woman to walk alone. After another semester passed, bringing him close to graduation, he was called for duty in the Army. He left for the front lines in Germany carrying a heavy heart for the one he didn't protect. He fell in combat, giving his life to the Allies' efforts to defeat the Nazis. Local legend has it that in spirit he returned to the place of his transgression. Believers claim that his soul suffered great guilt over the events of that fateful evening. Had he waited near the hat room as he did after every other performance, he could have stepped alongside her as she headed home. The two would have enjoyed each other's company on the brief walk. He could have joined the party later. Now, his spirit is allegedly stuck in a kind of cosmic loop, trying to right his perceived wrong. Eyeing males with suspicion, his spirit instead exudes warmth and protection to females who now inhabit the space.

Having occasionally been spotted as a beige mist resembling the form of a young man, he was given the moniker "Man-in-Tan."

Although the theaters this man performed in are long gone, he apparently isn't. Anonymous reports gathered from those who frequent the space today (including staff, students and visitors) claim mysterious knocks, bangs, doors opening and closing on their own and other phenomena of a classic haunting.

The Legend and the Hero

Now that we know a bit about the alleged haunting of this seemingly nondescript lobby in one of BGSU's historic buildings, it's time to turn our gaze backward a few decades. The lore surrounding the woman killed on her way home points to specific elements of the main character. The story goes that during the 1940s, one student was a prolific performer. He enlisted for service in World War II just as he was about to complete his college degree. He gave his life in combat, fighting German forces. As a student, he was kind, courteous and considerate of his fellow performers, with a special focus on protecting those of the female persuasion. A product of the thinking of that time, this folktale centers on the view of

One section of the Veteran's Memorial located west of BGSU's Jerome Library (*background*). Robert M. Berardi's name is included.

women as dependent and vulnerable. It depicts their male counterparts as charged with the duty of safeguarding them. These values have evolved to some extent with the advent of women's liberation. But in the 1940s, this movement had yet to surface.

An in-depth search of historical records that might fit this tale's claims was unable to produce any records of a young female student being assaulted and killed during this time. So this aspect of the story is very likely conjecture. Lore of all kinds is rife with tantalizing details created to draw the listener in. More engaging plots pull on sympathies to generate a sense of urgency. It's the stuff of great storytellers, from Williams Shakespeare to Stephen King. A good yarn requires many things. Chief among them is the engaged sympathy of the listener.

It's true that no records reflect the murder of a defenseless co-ed at that time. Remarkably, though, the historical record contains uncanny details about a young BGSU male student whose known life reflects the facts of the tale's protagonist. His untimely and self-sacrificing death was publicly mourned. He was memorialized in local newspapers. His name is inscribed on memorials on BGSU's campus. It is included among many other names of BGSU students who lost their lives in service to the United States.

Folktales that center on paranormal claims are typically a mix of fiction and fact. They reflect our attempts as humans to make sense of our existence, our vulnerabilities and what it means to lose the best and brightest among us. When a community suffers the loss of a young person full of vitality and promise, we grasp for answers. The Man-in-Tan ghost story reflects our need to keep those brightest of souls alive in our collective memory.

Often, despite all the conjecture, legendary tales like this are seeded by some kernel of truth. With some excavation of historical data, one often finds a narrative even more compelling than the paranormal claims. Such is the case with this subject. What follows is the true story of a young man who gave his life in the service of enduring freedoms. His story is presented in honor of that sacrifice. It is *not* presented with the aim of associating him with the alleged spiritual activity that still occurs. Rather, the intention in sharing his story is to shine a light on what was lost in his death and how we might learn from his life.

ROBERT M. BERARDI

Robert Berardi was born on March 21, 1922, in the little-known mountainous microstate the Republic of San Marino, a landlocked nation within northern Italy. It is still today among the world's oldest and smallest republics, encompassing an area of less than twenty-five square miles. But at the time of his birth, political elements that had been brewing since World War I were beginning to boil over. Jobs and resources were scarce, resulting in increased tensions among socioeconomic classes. This provided fertile

Artist's illustration of Robert M. Berardi based on U.S. Army photo, enlisted April 3, 1943.

ground for the growing fascist sentiment that preyed on fears that the lower classes would rise in rebellion.

It was in this milieu that the Berardi family lived a modest life as farmers. Father Adam and mother Teresa would add two children to the family after Robert. Leonello "Nello" arrived in 1925, followed by a daughter, Erma, in 1927. This young family with humble roots lived in a tiny country surrounded by Benito Mussolini's menacing politics of nationalism and military might. These forces likely contributed to the family's decision to leave in the summer of 1927. With their youngest less than six months old, the Berardi family traveled to Genoa to board the SS *Conte Biancamano*. The Berardi family was likely among the ship's 2,600 passengers in third class. At only five years old, Robert must have wondered at the shiny new ocean liner's splendor. Having just been launched in 1925, it was equipped with two steam engines that allowed for a top speed of twenty knots. It carried the Berardi family to their destination, the port of New York City, on July 29, 1927.

Three years later, in 1930, U.S. Census records show that the Berardi family had settled in Sandusky, Ohio. Adam Berardi had taken a job as a laborer at a local stone quarry. The family of five had also welcomed Adam's sister, brother-in-law and niece into their modest Sandusky home. It appears his brother in-law also got a job at the quarry. Perhaps to help make ends meet, Adam had taken in a coworker as a lodger in the home. The place, listed at 313 McKelvey Street, was surely cramped with ten people living under one roof. But the men had jobs and a means to put food on the table. The occupants were far removed from the rising threat of totalitarianism in their native country.

Moving forward another ten years, the 1940 Census records show the Berardi family still in Sandusky. They had moved to 434 Finch Street, a cute corner lot with a single-family home that stands today. By that time, eighteen-year-old Robert was about to finish high school. Both parents had taken up employment with a local rubber factory. They became part of a larger cause to support the war effort with needed rubber-manufacturing capacity. No doubt the steady income allowed this immigrant family's ascendency into the middle class. Nello and Erma also attended public schools and were undoubtedly assimilating into American ways of life.

After receiving his high school diploma, Robert began his college career at BGSU, pursuing a degree in business administration and accounting. He wasted no time claiming his role on campus as an energetic, creative force with which to be reckoned. Just a few months into his freshman year, he was famous for his involvement in a campus group called the Merry Minstrel Men. It included Robert and several of his fellow dorm residents at Kohl Hall. At the time, this blackface comedy routine was well received on campus. Today, we see these acts for the racist tropes they promoted. But at the time, these performances were lauded and helped propel Robert's fame on campus. He had superhuman skills when it came to the accordion. He used the jewel-studded instrument to woo audiences from the stage. Many audiences pleaded for encores. By January 1942, he was performing live on WFIN, a radio station out of Findlay. Soon his performance schedule was booked to capacity.

Robert was a consummate student, attaining excellent marks across academic domains. His name frequented the Dean's List. Even more than this, he participated in nearly every facet of campus life. He was a news reporter, sports editor and advertising manager for the *Bee Gee News*. He was a student advisor and a member of the Glee Club and the Debate Team. By May 1942, he had been voted sophomore representative to Student Council following a campus-wide election.

A Life Interrupted

Amid all his success and his small-town fame and accolades, Robert Berardi astonished once more. Only three months after being voted vice-president of Pi Kappa Alpha fraternity, he chose to enlist in the U.S. Army. It was April 1943. At the time, most college students received a deferment from the draft. Robert, who by all counts had blossomed into an entertainer lauded by the masses, willingly walked away from it all. Near the end of his junior year, he volunteered to fight for the country that had taken in his family at their time of need. This immigrant, this bright young scholar, this celebrated entertainer, this burgeoning leader weighed his own needs and desires against those of his adopted country.

In an act of supreme sacrifice, he turned to a life of service. Perhaps he understood all too well that the precious freedoms he'd come to enjoy could only be preserved by fighting for them.

World War II draft card of Robert M. Berardi. *National Archives at St. Louis; St. Louis, Missouri; Draft Registration Cards for Ohio, 10/16/1940-03/31/1947; Record Group: Records of the Selective Service System, 147; Box: 99.*

After passing a physical exam at the Toledo Induction Center, he and a group of other enlistees were sent to Camp Perry in Port Clinton for basic training. On their departure from a Toledo railway station, a large number of family and friends gathered to send them off. Led by Reverend Louis Quade, pastor of the local Methodist church, the group shared fervent prayers that their boys fight valiantly and return home. Members of the VFW distributed candies and smokes while shaking the new soldiers' hands. Members of the American Legion distributed small Bibles. All stood and watched as the train shoved off, its mournful whistle carrying with it the hopes and fears of so many, including one hardworking, now thoroughly American, Berardi family.

Once basic training was complete, Robert was sent to the University of Utah in Salt Lake City. His intellectual skills and natural leadership abilities placed him in line for specialized Army training. By the following November, he had returned to the Midwest, at a station in Lafayette, Indiana, before heading to another training station at Camp Swift, Texas. There he awaited final orders for deployment to the European theater. At least that is what he assumed at the time. The months plodded along as his anxious wait for the next step stretched out.

It was at this time that Robert's eighteen-year-old brother, Nello, decided to follow in his big brother's footsteps. He enlisted after receiving his high school diploma. Remarkably, Nello was the first of the brothers to see active combat. After about a year of training and stateside assignments, he joined the Army's Seventh Infantry Regiment, Third Infantry Division. He took part in what later became known as Operation Diadem. This Allied offensive was launched in May 1944 as part of the Italian campaign to break German defenses around Rome. The mission was also purposed to tie down German forces that could otherwise have been sent to France.

Left: Artist's illustration of Nello Berardi, based on a U.S. Army photo. He enlisted on July 10, 1943.

Right: Artist's illustration of Nello Berardi's gravestone in Sicily-Rome American Cemetery and Memorial, Nettuno, Lazio, Italy.

World War II draft card of Nello Berardi. *National Archives at St. Louis; St. Louis, Missouri; Draft Registration Cards for Ohio, 10/16/1940-03/31/1947; Record Group: Records of the Selective Service System, 147; Box: 99.*

The distraction was necessary to limit German forces as the Allies were preparing for the D-Day invasion.

Nello fell while taking part in a sortie from the Anzio beachhead on May 24, 1944. He was struck by enemy fire, which left a gaping wound in his abdomen. After only six months of active combat service, nineteen-year-old Nello Berardi succumbed to his wounds in an Allied hospital in Italy. He survived for four days before breathing his last only a short distance from his birthplace, the Republic of San Marino. Robert received word of his only brother's death while stationed in Camp Swift, Texas. He had not yet been actively deployed.

Despite the family's tragedy, Operation Diadem was considered an Allied victory. The German lines were breeched, forcing their troops to retreat northwestward.

The Last Full Measure of Devotion

Four months later, in September 1944, Robert's extended period of specialist training finally ended. He was assigned to the 102nd Infantry Division, 407th Infantry Regiment. This unit arrived in the United Kingdom and entered active combat just a few weeks later. They were sent into the crucible of the war: Nazi-occupied Germany and central Europe. By the ripe old age of twenty-two, Robert had been promoted to sergeant.

The first foray of the 102nd into the European theater was at Cherbourg, France, for a brief training period before officially confronting hostiles. Through October and into November, they joined forces with other divisions leading an offensive campaign into German-occupied territory. By the end of November 1944, Sergeant Berardi and his fellow soldiers had staged attacks along the Roer River. Their success allowed them control of this crucial German waterway, providing a vital advantage for later operations that would lend the Allies even more ground.

All these efforts led to what was then known as Operation Grenade.

Operation Grenade was a strategic effort to cross the Roer between Roermond, Netherlands, and Düren, Germany. This decisive campaign marked the beginning of the Allied invasion of Germany, a turning point near the end of the war. U.S. forces were to cross into Germany and join Canadian forces arriving from fresh victories in the Netherlands. But when the Germans saw the Canadian troops advancing, they opened up sluice gates of the Roer's upstream dams. This flooded the plains, dashing the Americans' plans for a successful crossing.

The area remained flooded for two weeks, during which time Hitler did not allow his field commanders to withdraw. He believed a battle was inevitable and that German troops should fight honorably to protect their fatherland. The conflict soon began. Various forces of the U.S. Ninth Army finally set foot on German soil, on the eastern bank of the Roer.

Members of Company B, First Battalion, 407th Regiment, 102nd Division, February 21, 1945, Gereonsweiler, Germany, three days before Robert Berardi's death. *U.S. National Archives, U.S. Army Signal Corps.*

By the end of this bloody battle, Germans suffered 90,000 casualties; the Allies, 23,000. Sergeant Robert Berardi was one of them. He had survived five full months, through the fall and the better part of winter. But by his regiment's 173rd day of active combat, he would be listed among its troops killed in action.

He gave his life in the Allies' final efforts to bring the war home to the Nazis. It was here the Allies began to establish domination over all of Europe.

The accompanying photo shows some of Robert's fellow soldiers mugging for the camera. Taken in Gereonsweiler, Germany, on a staged dude ranch dubbed "El Rancho," it reflects the typical American swagger no doubt stirred by their successive victories. It was taken on February 21, 1945, three days before Robert's death, on a farm fewer than five kilometers from where he would be killed. Could one of these jubilant GIs be him?

THE TERRIBLE NEWS ARRIVES

A couple of weeks passed before word of Robert's death on February 24, 1945, reached home. The Berardis had the distinct burden of being the first Sandusky family to lose two sons to the war. The news soon spread across the communities of Sandusky and Bowling Green. The *Bee Gee News* published an article recalling Robert's contributions to university life and the sacrifices he made in walking away from the completion of his degree. Several local and regional newspapers published his photo and obituary.

Artist's illustration of Robert Berardi's gravestone in Netherlands American Cemetery, Margraten, Netherlands.

In the decades since, Robert Berardi is still remembered. His name is memorialized in BGSU's Memorial Hall and at the Veteran's Memorial outside Jerome Library. And within the community of Sandusky, a stone memorial bearing his and other veterans' names stands at Veterans Memorial Park downtown. In addition, both Robert and Nello's names are included on a bronze plaque hanging on a wall in the Sandusky High School cafeteria.

Sergeant Berardi's final resting place can be found among more than eight thousand graves at the Netherlands American Cemetery in Margraten, Netherlands. It is the only cemetery within Dutch borders for American war dead from World War II.

IN SUMMARY

Robert Berardi's influence on the world during his brief twenty-two-year life is impressive, to say the least. He'd taken the campus by storm on arriving at BGSU in 1940. He was a consummate performer, scholar and leader. It's a path that would have assuredly taken him to even greater heights on completing his degree. Perhaps it was this stellar reputation that made it so difficult for those who came to know and love him to accept his tragic passing. Perhaps an effort to make sense of something so painful led to a kind of storytelling we humans are prone to doing in our own minds.

In any case, many of the traits of the oral folktale of the "Man-in-Tan" ghost at University Hall came to resemble those of the very real Robert Berardi. The protagonist in the ghost story encapsulates what it means to love, perform, protect and sacrifice for others. Those traits, at least, reflect what can be known of the young man who once lived, studied and performed on these campus grounds.

There is certainly no way of connecting the alleged paranormal activity at this spot to one person. And more to the point, some may feel that it is dishonorable to suggest that this Purple Heart recipient is now a lost spirit wandering the halls of a historic structure. We'll never know for sure what accounts for the unexplained experiences, much less whether they emanate from the essence of one deceased person. Despite this, one piece of good fortune is clear. These mysterious happenings led to further investigation of the story's claims. The research that followed brought forth a true story worth remembering.

May Sergeant Robert Berardi's influence remain not only at BGSU, but also on you, dear reader. May we give freely of our talents for causes greater than ourselves.

May we value the freedoms he and his brother gave all to protect.

2
FOR EDMUND KEEP(S)

Very few of us are what we seem.
—Agatha Christie

The city of Bowling Green, the seat of Wood County, is known for its quaint downtown. Among the buildings that run primarily down Main Street are artsy establishments like the independent coffee shop Grounds for Thought. Iconic bars and eateries line the strip, each with its own character and charm. Many of these businesses are housed in historic buildings constructed during Bowling Green's "Boom Era" of the late 1800s and early 1900s. These treasured structures are so well loved that this section of street was placed in the National Register of Historic Places in May 1987. Ground levels of these historic buildings have been renovated many times over to accommodate the commercial needs of twenty-first-century customers. But many upper floors of the multistory structures are largely unchanged.

The history that these buildings contain, the way they beckon shoppers back to simpler times, is certainly one draw for visitors and locals alike. Just beyond their beauty and allure lies a compelling tale, specific to the 100 block of South Main. This very real story had almost been forgotten, lost in the blur of decades gone by. Although most Bowling Green residents have never heard of this gripping 1918 murder case, those who own and work in the buildings have sensed something of the apparent spirits who remain. Some believe that these unexplained entities yearn for their stories to be known.

View of Bowling Green's Main Street, looking south, September 2022.

View of Bowling Green's Main Street, looking north, September 2022.

Left: For Keeps gift shop, 144 South Main Street, Bowling Green, Ohio, September 2022.

Below: Hankey Building housing Beckett's Burger Bar, 163 South Main Street, Bowling Green, Ohio, September 2022.

One such person is Amy Craft Ahrens, proprietor of the For Keeps gift store at 144 South Main. She and her father opened the retail space in 1997. Their aim was to provide the community with an eclectic array of options for gift giving. For Keeps has been voted Best Gift Store in Wood County for more than a decade. While its retail success is unquestioned, it seems the enchanting shop houses more than trinkets and keepsakes. Shortly after purchasing the building about twenty-six years ago, Amy and multiple employees encountered evidence of the ghost they have affectionately come to refer to as "Frank."

Within weeks of moving in, staff could hear Frank walking the length of the second floor, even though no one was there. These steps are heard yet today. Objects are knocked around and set ajar, including framed pictures on walls. There was something about Thomas Kincade that Frank didn't appreciate. For some reason, only Kincade prints have been turned askew. And on one occasion, a Kincade print was removed from its hook on the wall and placed face down on the floor. Music boxes, which require opening to play, mysteriously open themselves, setting cheerful yet eerie tunes playing for no one. Ghostly moans are a common occurrence, especially after closing, when staff members are alone and locking up for the night. Amy's most memorable experience occurred late one evening when she distinctly heard her own name, "Aaaammmyyyy," in a singsong tone wafting from thin air.

These unexplained encounters tend to come sporadically, perhaps every two to three months. Just when things settle back into a normal routine, Frank resurfaces to remind others of his presence. And For Keeps isn't the only establishment with a reputation for unexplained experiences. Across the street, the J.R. Hankey Building abounds in claims of disembodied laughter, lights turning on and off on their own and the distinct sound of something heavy being dragged across the unused upper floor. Built in 1892, this three-story structure has served many purposes. In recent decades, it has housed restaurants. Its current owners acquired the building at 163 South Main to open Beckett's Burger Bar, a beloved eatery for locals and visitors alike.

THE TRUTH BEHIND THE LORE

For some time, local lore has held that a murder took place on the third floor of the Hankey building, which was rumored to have been a theater. It was assumed that the spirit of some ill-fated thespian was to blame for the unexplained occurrences. Few records about the use of this space as a theater have been found. However, another story, one with as many twists and turns as any good stage drama, has been discovered. Keep reading.

The weekend finally arrived one brisk Saturday night in February 1918. As usual, Edmund Keep was managing the gambling den he'd founded above Prier's Hardware. He moved quickly among card tables, supplying eager gamblers with chips so the playing could proceed uninterrupted. The steady rhythm kept men engaged, bringing little time for contemplation on their dwindling chances to salvage their paychecks. Weekends brought a steady increase in business and a need to keep his clientele satisfied. This meant carrying no less than $100 in small bills (about $1,800 today). Keep made a rule for himself never to play. This helped avoid any hard feelings among players suffering punishing losses. This retired electric railcar operator had discovered his newfound talent for providing "entertainment." Bowling Green proved the perfect spot, a rural midwestern town short on recreation and long on workingmen's leisure time. The change of career invigorated Keep. His success was undeniable, both in terms of revenue and social standing. That his gambling den existed at all was not a well-kept secret among residents at large. With a roll of the eyes, even members of polite society and law enforcement shrugged off the enterprise.

Despite this, there existed in Keep a growing unease. He was jovial enough, as any person must be in the recreation business. Yet there was tension that his nervous laughter couldn't conceal. F.W. Munn, one of his regular customers, recalled to reporters an instance of Keep's vulnerability that he just couldn't shake. One evening, the usual convivial look in Keep's eyes vanished as the two men sat down to watch a game at play near the rear of the gaming room.

Inside view of the third floor of the Hankey building. This space housed Edmund Keep's illegal gambling den in the early 1900s. Photo taken in September 2022.

Keep leaned into Munn and, in hushed tones, shared his concerns about Floyd Houser. In recent weeks, Houser had frequented the den more and more as his zealous desperation grew. This was not unusual for regular customers. Lots of men were known to grow frantic as they chased their mounting losses. But there was something different about Houser.

Keep had confided to Munn in a rare moment of candor. It was something in Houser's gruff manner, directed at Keep, that was worrisome. The tone revealed Houser as a loose cannon. Keep admitted he wanted Houser to stop coming altogether, but he was afraid to prohibit him outright, as it might provoke the very aggression he was trying to avoid. Munn was surprised at Keep's admission and asked for more details on the threat he was facing. And just like that, Keep made an about-face, dismissing his own statements and claiming himself too sensitive on the whole matter. With that he stood, moving on to the next table, leaving Munn perplexed.

A couple weeks later, on the night of February 16, 1918, that confusing exchange still weighed on Munn's mind. Keep had seemed a bit nervous earlier in the evening. Houser had been there, losing all of the sixteen dollars he'd brought with him. After displaying a sour, withdrawn mood, Houser finally left, much to Keep's relief. But his nervousness remained. Keep skittered from one poker table to the next and then to the window overlooking the street-level entrance. His apparent state of distraction boiled over on miscalculating one gambler's buy-in. The customer, unhappy with being shortchanged, pointed out the indiscretion loud enough for all to hear. Keep deferred at once, apologizing, then threw in a couple extra chips to make up for it. As awkward as it was, the whole mix-up served to break the spell for a bit. Keep regained his composure in a way that brought him back to his cheerful self. Perhaps that's why he didn't hear the street-level entrance door slam open with a bang. It was followed by the sound of footsteps running up the stairway.

Having apparently lost his nervousness, Keep didn't seem to hear the commotion. Players called his attention to the noise, causing him to check a side entrance door. No one was there when he opened it. He then went into the next room (an unoccupied bedroom for rent), which led to the den's main entrance. Keep quickly opened the door. Whoever stood on the other side was shrouded in darkness. The light above the landing, which always shone down on the space in front of the door, had somehow been extinguished.

A muffled gunshot rang out as soon as he opened the door. On hearing it, players rushed toward him and watched as Keep stumbled backward several steps before resting on a small bed.

"The son-of-a-bitch shot me!" he exclaimed as heavy footsteps rumbled down the stairs. The bottom door slammed open. Some gamblers ran to Keep's side, gasping at the blood oozing from his stomach. Others peered down the darkened stairway, seeing nothing. One man walking down the street named Edmund Hopkins, however, had a perfect view. He was coming home that night from Potter's Dance Hall and looked across the street as one assailant came bounding out of the entrance, falling on his hands and knees. The second assailant came right after him, toppling over as the two scurried back to their feet. The second man had an overcoat wrapped over his right forearm, concealing whatever he held in his hand. It all happened so fast, and in the dark, that Hopkins didn't get a good enough look at their faces.

A panic set in upstairs as players dispersed. One man had gone to tell the cops, finding Officer John Shoecraft. He then phoned Dr. I.M. Shrader, who arrived on the scene within minutes. Keep screamed with pain and asked "for God's sake" to give him something for it. Dr. Shrader did so before beginning an emergency procedure to remove the bullet from his back. It had lodged about three inches from his spine, nearly going clean through him. It entered at the stomach and stopped only a quarter of an inch below the skin on his back. Keep grew hazy from the blood loss. Fearing time was running out, Dr. Shrader asked repeated questions as to the identity of the guilty party.

"It was a short, heavy-set man wearing a cap," Keep replied. He had no enemies, no one he knew who wanted him dead. Dr. Schrader leveled with him, acknowledging that death was imminent. If Keep had any clue as to who might have done this, he would have to say so now.

Keep fell silent.

Moments later, a young boy discovered an unattended blue cap, size six and seven-eighths, lying on Prospect Street.

By 2:00 a.m., Sheriff Gus Skibbie had arrived at the home of Floyd Houser. Initial interviews from witnesses on the scene placed Houser there earlier that evening. Sheriff Skibbie knew that Houser had left only forty-five minutes before the shooting took place. He also knew of Houser's wholesale loss that day of $16 (equivalent to $300 today). On facing the sheriff's pointed questions, Houser rose to the occasion. He offered to help in any way he could. Yes, indeed, he had lost all the cash he brought, but that certainly hadn't been the first time. Houser admitted his poker skills left much to be desired. He was sure the "fellas" would confirm that he'd suffered losses on numerous nights. None of those losses had led to murder, not even a scuffle.

Edmund Keep's grave site at Oak Grove Cemetery, Bowling Green, Ohio.

After leaving the poker game that night, Houser claimed to have played one quick game of pool before heading home and going to bed. He'd been sleeping when Sheriff Skibbie knocked on his door. He knew nothing of the events of the shooting. With no evidence to keep him, Houser was released.

The hunt was on to find the assailants as an investigation ensued. The light that normally illuminated the top of the stairway had been tampered with. This murder of a beloved and cheerful man had been planned. At the time, electric railcars ran from Bowling Green to Woodville, Tontogany and North Baltimore. Keep had been a fixture on the rail line, an accomplished motorman. Many who commuted on the service knew him well. Men of all sorts, fellow gamblers, day laborers and physicians, joined in a posse of sorts, scouring the town for the culprits. Their efforts proved fruitless. After a couple of days of searching and exhaustive interviews of everyone present, no viable leads resulted. No further arrests were made. Officials were unable to find a motive for the crime. Autopsy results indicated that the assailant shot Keep at point-blank range from the waistline. The gun had been so close that traces of powder were found on Keep's clothing.

The Simonds Family, Once Respected

Frank Simonds was born in Bowling Green on November 13, 1895. He and his family lived at 302 Reed Avenue, according to the 1910 U.S. Census. This simple, two-story, corner-lot home still stands today. Back then, it was owned free and clear by Frank's father, Jay Simonds, the master carpenter who presumably built it in 1900. Jay developed ambitions beyond his roles as husband and father to Frank and his two siblings, Fred and Gennell. The Simonds family name would soon carry prominence. Even though he failed at winning the Sheriff's position in 1890, Jay Simonds went on to win a city council seat in 1903. It was a role his firstborn son, Fred, would assume on reaching adulthood as well.

Jay and Rena Simonds's second child, Frank, had different ambitions from his older brother. He preferred the satisfaction of working with his hands. Together, he and his father founded Simonds and Son, the most sought-after carpentry business in all of Wood County. This established Frank as a carpenter in his own right in the community. The Simonds family by all appearances was respectable, serving the public with their talents in both carpentry and civil service.

At twenty-two years old, Frank's fateful decision would change all that.

A Mystery Solved

The murder of Edmund Keep was still unsolved in early November 1923. By then, most Bowling Green residents believed the trail had grown so cold that the guilty parties would never be found. Although the case had begun to fade in the public's memory, it certainly hadn't faded for one man.

Floyd Houser.

The gruff, petulant young man who had spooked poor Keep in the weeks before his death had since moved to Lima. Apparently down on his luck and looking for an easy way to score some cash, Houser plotted an extortion scheme. He reached out to an old Bowling Green acquaintance, Guy Danforth. Danforth was to deliver an unsigned letter to Fred Simonds, Frank's older brother and a revered City Councilman. The letter demanded that Fred meet with the unnamed author (Houser) at a rail station in Toledo. Cryptic yet demanding, the letter offered no details as to the purpose of the meeting. All that was made clear was that if Councilman Simonds did not present himself at the specified time and place, consequences "of life and death" would result.

The letter was followed by a telegram conveying the same message and then a telephone call. It was this final point of contact when Houser boiled over. Perhaps Fred Simonds guessed his identity, or perhaps Houser's infamous temper got the best of him. In any case, he revealed himself in a tirade. By then, Fred Simonds had had enough. Houser's hothead reputation from years ago was not easily forgotten. He decided to bring the matter to Wood County Sheriff Ervin Reitzel's attention.

Houser had skipped town shortly after Keep's murder in February 1918. Even though nearly six years had passed, his reputation remained well known in Bowling Green. Houser was the only person to have been arrested in connection with Keep's death. No doubt, the sheriff believed his obscure demands to meet Fred Simonds had something to do with the unsolved murder. Sheriff Reitzel arranged for a sting operation. Keeping out of sight, he and two Toledo police officers lay in wait at the Toledo rail station during the planned rendezvous. All were surprised when Guy Danforth showed up at the station to tell Fred Simonds that Houser changed the meeting place at the last minute. He was now waiting for him at a poolroom down the street.

In an instant, the lawmen stepped forward, arresting Danforth on the spot. After he was in custody, they proceeded to the poolroom and summarily arrested Houser without incident. A long and grueling interrogation ensued, which eventually broke through Houser's cocky façade. He admitted that the purpose of the whole enterprise was extortion. He planned to threaten Fred Simonds with the release of evidence that implicated his brother Frank in the 1918 unsolved murder of Edmund Keep.

In confessing to the attempted extortion, Houser dug himself deeper into self-incrimination on the issue of Keep's murder. With pressure mounting from the officer's unrelenting questions, he finally cracked. Houser confessed that he and his friend, Frank Simonds, had been planning to rob Keep's gambling den for some time before finally attempting it on February 16, 1918. The operation got the green light once they convinced a third party, a man named Vernon Rhodaberger, for assistance. The three men planned to hold up the place. This meant robbing not only Keep himself but his gamblers as well. The group donned masks to conceal their identities. But when the moment arrived to rush up the stairway, Houser got cold feet. Furious, Rhodaberger scolded Houser as he removed his cap and gave it to him to hold. Houser waited nervously at the bottom entrance as the other two men ran up the stairs to the third floor. Houser ran off when he heard the gunshot. He recalled dropping Rhodaberger's cap on South Prospect Street as he fled; the same cap was found by a passing boy the next day.

The crime had gone unsolved for six years. The trio would have likely gotten off scot-free if it weren't for Houser's greedy, clumsy attempt at blackmail. In the end, he was done in by his own ineptitude, the same force that ensnared his accomplices.

Vernon Rhodaberger was twenty years old at the time of the murder. Originally from Sharon, Pennsylvania, he became a transient after losing a semipro pitching position. Simonds and Houser had been friends for some time when Rhodaberger showed up in Bowling Green looking for work. When they approached him with the scheme, he agreed to it on the spot. After the botched robbery, Rhodaberger fled back to Sharon. In an effort to make an honest living, he found work as a sign maker and lived in a boardinghouse. Perfectly law-abiding, the now twenty-six-year-old found love, proposing to his landlady's daughter. The course correction young Rhodaberger was trying to make came to an abrupt halt when Sheriff Reitzel traveled 180 miles to arrest him. After the sheriff knocked on the boardinghouse door, Rhodaberger stood up from the dinner table exclaiming that he knew why the lawman was there.

He was arrested without incident.

OUR FRANK SIMONDS

And that brings us to Frank Simonds, the man who pulled the trigger. This Bowling Green native, son of a master carpenter and civic leader, also skipped town shortly after the deed was done. His intention was to enlist in the Army. It would be his third attempt at enlisting. He had been turned down during his first two tries, long before the murder. Records listed him as "physically unfit" to serve. By the late winter of 1918, however, the Army had loosened its standards, accepting most anyone willing to sign up. The nation's involvement in the Great War had been dragging on for nearly a year. Records show that Simonds successfully enlisted with the army on April 1, 1918, less than two months after Keep's murder.

This might have seemed like a surefire way to get out of town as the investigation gathered steam. But what awaited Simonds on the other side of the Atlantic were the dismal and hopeless trenches on the battlefields of France. He fought in the Meuse-Argonne Offensive, the final offensive campaign for the Allies. This seven-week operation became the single-deadliest battle in U.S. history, resulting in 350,000 casualties. The young troops who fought it were mostly inexperienced, resulting in fatal errors all over the battlefield. In addition, the lethal Spanish Flu pandemic spread rampantly among soldiers living in the cramped conditions of the trenches.

It's hard to imagine the horrors and trauma he faced. That Simonds survived the ordeal is a miracle unto itself. Yet what is most intriguing are brief mentions in local newspapers of his receiving two citations for bravery. He held a distinguished record for marksmanship and fidelity to his duties as a soldier. Frustratingly, no further details on just what he did can be found. A request for his service record from military archives proved fruitless. Tragically, most service records of World War I veterans were destroyed during a fire at the National Personnel Center in 1973. One can only imagine what brave steps this murderer might have taken to try to atone for the life he'd taken back home.

By the grace of God, Private First Class Simonds survived his deployment and sailed for home aboard the *America* out of Brest, France, on March 28, 1919. He arrived in Boston nine days later. After finally returning to his hometown of Bowling Green, he lived with his parents, younger sister, maternal grandfather and aunt. By now all leads on Keep's murder had subsided, making Simonds's stay in Bowling Green less risky. He'd gone back to work in his father's carpentry business. Historical documents indicate that he was becoming a businessman in his own right. By May 1922, he'd formed a partnership with H.T. Clague and opened a concrete building block plant. Theirs was the first of its kind in Bowling Green, establishing a monopoly on new concrete construction.

Perhaps Simonds hoped he'd set himself on the right path. Perhaps he hoped his sacrifices during war might have paid off some of the cosmic debt he owed. Whatever his state of mind, several written accounts describe his reaction to finally being arrested for the crime on December 1, 1923. He admitted right away that he was the one who shot Edmund Keep. Simonds had had no hard feelings toward the owner of the gambling den. He acknowledged that Houser's get-rich-quick scheme had appealed to him when he learned how much cash passed hands every night in the joint. The two knew they'd need a third man to join them to help cover the bases. When the young, eager out-of-towner Vernon Rhodaberger showed up, he fit the bill perfectly. The plan was for all three of them to burst in. The element of surprise would be in their favor as they demanded money from stunned players. When Houser lost his gumption at the last minute, Simonds and Rhodaberger pressed on up the stairs, with Simonds gripping a .38-caliber revolver in his pocket. The plan went awry when Keep, himself, flung open the door at the top, blocking their entry just as they were about to burst in. In a moment of impulsive confusion, Simonds squeezed off the shot that felled Keep, the man who by Munn's account had sensed something bad was about to happen.

Stunned at what they had done, both Simonds and Rhodaberger abandoned the planned robbery and fled down the darkened stairs. They toppled over each other on reaching the street below and had to regain their footing before fleeing through the streets. Houser, having stayed at the bottom of the stairs the whole time, took off as soon as he'd heard the gunshot.

On Monday, December 3, 1923, Wood County Prosecutor Ray Avery arraigned first-degree murder charges against all three suspects. Although all of them had made verbal confessions to police on their arrests, they pleaded not guilty. This is not uncommon in capital murder cases, as not guilty pleas are often mandatory at arraignment. All three were bound over to the grand jury without bond. By early January, all three had been indicted on both first- and second-degree murder charges.

Perhaps in an effort to spare Keep's family the trauma of a trial, plea bargains were offered to the defendants. Simonds eventually accepted a guilty plea of second-degree murder. Newspaper reporters noted an apparent attitude of calm relief that settled over him after his plea was formally entered. This young Bowling Green entrepreneur, a war hero and confessed murderer, was sentenced to life in the Ohio Penitentiary.

In a stunning development, Rhodaberger was tried separately. Many character witnesses came forward from his hometown, proclaiming his kind nature and law-abiding character. This effort by his legal defense was combined with Simonds's shocking testimony that he and Houser never fully informed Rhodaberger of their intentions to rob the place. This proved convincing enough for the prosecutor to drop the charge against him to manslaughter, to which Rhodaberger pleaded. He was sentenced to between five and twenty years in prison.

Floyd Houser, having schemed the whole event from the start, also accepted a plea of manslaughter. He received a sentence of nineteen years in prison.

Frank Simonds's Final Chapter

Fortunately for the Simonds family, both of Frank's parents died before their son was indicted and sentenced for murder. His mother, Rena (Hullibarger)

Simonds, died of pneumonia on January 5, 1922. Frank's well-respected father, Jay Simonds, was victim of a horrific explosion while trying to thaw a gas regulator in his home. Although he survived the extensive burns, the fumes he inhaled severely damaged his lungs, resulting in his eventual death on January 6, 1923. Both mother and father likely went to their graves viewing their middle son as a war hero and burgeoning entrepreneur following in his father's footsteps.

Less than a year after his father's death, Frank Simonds's world came to a screeching halt when his old friend, Floyd Houser, put into motion a "brilliant" criminal extortion scheme. The cards fell quickly.

One might think this is the end of a tragic and convoluted story. And yet, one scene remains.

Come December 1926, a great effort had been set in motion asking for the governor's pardon of Frank Simonds. Multiple prominent members of the community sent letters to Governor Victor Donahay's office on the young man's behalf, citing his bravery in battle. Knowing that he risked his own life to save others, many Bowling Green residents argued that he'd paid his debt to society. Others remarked on his skills in the carpentry trade and his efforts to bring a new industry (concrete construction) to the region. Even

Frank Simonds's modest grave site at Oak Grove Cemetery, Bowling Green, Ohio.

Judge McClelland, the man who sentenced him to life in prison, got swept up in the community-wide effort for his release. He wrote a letter to the governor as well.

And just as the movement was reaching a crescendo, Simonds contracted appendicitis, requiring surgery. Reports indicate that he had been a model prisoner up until being stricken with the illness. He was just approaching the start of his third year in prison when the procedure to remove his appendix, which was meant to save his life, took it. This man who survived the bloodiest battle in all of U.S. history and was awarded for his bravery in it—this man who took the life of Edmund Keep—died from complications of a routine medical procedure.

All this just as he was about to receive a pardon for his crime.

Frank Simonds would breathe his last inside the hospital wing of the Ohio Penitentiary on December 22, 1926. His body was prepared for burial, then sent to the home of Fred Simonds in Bowling Green. A burial with full military rites was conducted at Oak Grove Cemetery.

Epilogue

The hauntings known to happen still today among structures within the 100 block of South Main Street have been a mystery to most residents over the decades. There's no way to prove that the spiritual activity is related to these specific events. But this history offers an uncanny explanation. Edmund Keep's gambling den, an illegal but tolerated enterprise of its day, was indeed operated out of upper floors of the Hankey building. Claims of disembodied sounds and voices, including footsteps and ghostly apparitions, have been reported by restaurant workers and customers for decades. And just across the street stands a pretty little gift shop. When its staff are asked how their resident ghost got the name *Frank*, no one is quite sure. The name seems to have materialized of its own accord.

It's fanciful to consider that something of the shadow of Frank Simonds, the complicated Bowling Green native who lived one hundred years ago, remains in this space. Is it possible that he still longs for redemption? Could the guilt of taking an innocent man's life pin him to the place where it happened? Despite all his efforts at atonement, despite his honors for bravery and the love of those who pleaded for his pardon, nothing could restore Edmund Keep. Perhaps the impacts of our actions remain long after we're gone. Perhaps the hurt we cause cannot be erased by our good deeds.

We should do them anyway.

If we believe in such things as ghosts—spiritual beings trapped between this world and the next—what might the spirit of Frank Simonds have thought on seeing a gift shop open just across the street from the Hankey building, named For Keeps of all things? Does he sometimes wander over to marvel at the trinkets, play the music boxes and whisper to the staff? Perhaps he longs to pay tribute to the memory of the man whose life he snuffed out for no good reason.

Will he ever come to terms with that most selfish act? It may be a decision that haunts him for eternity.

3

FORT MEIGS

SPIRITS OF THE WAR OF 1812

Prepare a noble death song for the day when you go over the great divide.
—Tecumseh

Along the southern bank of the Maumee River, in the bustling city of
Perrysburg, lies an Ohio state memorial known all too well by most
Wood County residents. A sprawling park totaling sixty-five acres
contains within it a life-size monument: a replica of an early nineteenth-
century century fortress. Rough, hand-hewn timbers outline the ten-acre
section of land on which once stood the impenetrable Fort Meigs. Visitors
to these sacred grounds need little imagination to immerse themselves in
the space. Through the painstaking work of state and local preservationists,
the fort was reconstructed on the original site in the late 1960s. Since then,
it has gone through multiple updates and restorations. Those who come
for a visit today are welcomed by a modern visitor's center offering exhibits
that introduce the remarkable history of the place. On exiting this museum
space, visitors follow a path to the imposing fortress and pass through its
heavy main entry gate.

Passing through the fortified gate offers visitors a chance to envision
themselves a soldier fighting to defend a nation in its infancy. In April 1813,
the United States was but thirty-seven years old. And in a real test of its
sovereignty, America was under siege. British and Native American forces
had allied in an effort to halt expansion into the Northwest Territory. A
crucial location within that expanding territory was the spot near the mouth

Left: Entry gate to Fort Meigs, May 2022.

Below: Satellite view of Fort Meigs. *Google Maps, imagery ©2022, Maxar Technologies, State of Ohio, OSIP, USDA/FPAC/GEO.*

of the great Maumee, the largest waterway that empties into Lake Erie. Whoever controlled this vital route controlled commerce and travel to points yet unsettled.

As the first year of the War of 1812 passed, things weren't looking good for the Americans. Successive defeats in battles all over the region suggested the fledging nation might collapse. The British troops were seasoned and better equipped; the Americans took heavy losses throughout the Northwest Territory. Many assumed the nation's brief experiment in democracy would soon end in defeat.

The attempted siege of Fort Meigs would prove pivotal.

AND SPIRITS REMAIN

Having only scratched the surface of this monumental history, let us take a moment to consider an even wider view. This site's historical significance is known to many. Beyond that, its reputation as a hotbed of spiritual activity has flourished for decades. It's grown so much, in fact, that a nonprofit organization, the Old Northwest Military History Association (ONMHA), sponsors yearly Garrison Ghost Walks of the fort. These often sold-out tours led by costumed actors offer tantalizing insights into otherworldly experiences sometimes reported by visitors and employees alike. Eerie, blue spherical lights are sometimes seen floating above the ground within the fort. The booming yet distant percussion of heavy cannons sometimes echo off the timbered walls. Disembodied footfalls, like those of a man running at full speed, are heard rushing toward unsuspecting visitors. And dramatic, full-bodied apparitions of soldiers clad in period military uniforms are sometimes spotted standing guard. Some believe that elaborate military reenactments, in full display year after year, are what keep the spirits active. Perhaps these lost souls get caught up in the theatrics. Perhaps they long to find some kind of resolution to the devastation they confronted in their final moments.

It appears that some soldiers have yet to be relieved of their duties. Let's consider the lore that has sprung up around these occurrences. Let's contemplate just what may have persuaded these spirits to linger in this space.

One common ghost story involves the image of a transparent soldier standing at an artillery battery. He most often appears standing before the cannon, at the break in the wall that allows artillery fire to pass through. Facing outward, he waves his arms in a panic. Those lucky enough to spot him for brief seconds before he fades claim his sense of urgency is palpable.

Artillery battery where a full-bodied ghost soldier has been spotted waving frantically.

Just what could have persuaded a soldier to expose himself in such a vulnerable position and then call such dramatic attention to himself? On the surface, such a scenario would seem a kind of death wish, a surrender to the trauma and futility of war. Could this shadowy figure be the remnant of a soldier who gave in to a despair wrought by exhaustion and desperation? Perhaps. However, another explanation offers intriguing insight into a crucial moment of the fabled siege. This man's apparent frantic flailing may not reflect an attempt at suicide but a valiant and selfless effort to save hundreds of lives. His ultimate failure to do so may be what imprisons him there today at this earthly place.

Let us consider a remarkable moment in the hellish saga of the Siege of Fort Meigs.

THE ILL-FATED KENTUCKIANS

The early morning of May 5, 1813, marked the start of the fifth day of the Siege of Fort Meigs by British and Native forces. The enemy had made camp in the ruins of Fort Miamis, located downriver on the opposite bank of the Maumee. American forces within Fort Meigs had somehow managed to hold up under constant barrage. Critical supplies were dwindling, including ammunitions, food and medicine. Even worse was the gnawing exhaustion setting in among the troops. Without some turn of fate, the situation for the Americans was growing bleaker by the moment.

Luckily, General William Henry Harrison, commander of the fort, had learned months earlier of Kentucky Governor Isaac Shelby's intentions to send troops to aid in the war effort. Knowing this, he began a correspondence with Shelby requesting a unit be sent to Fort Meigs. The governor obliged, instructing General Green Clay and his band of 1,200 Kentucky militiamen to march northward. Harrison's request proved prescient as the siege wore on. On May 2, one brave Fort Meigs soldier secreted himself out of the fort and into the wilderness. He eventually found his way to General Clay's troops. The Kentuckians were en route, not yet having reached Fort Meigs before the siege began.

The classified orders carried in the breast pocket of this unnamed courier informed General Clay of the desperate situation and the need for rapid reinforcements. Clay was to advance his troops forward while Harrison's men initiated a sortie from the fort. This would provide cover for the Kentuckians to spike the British cannons and then gain entry into the fort. Their arrival would finally bring relief to Harrison's exhausted troops.

The order was delivered in safety, leading Clay to dispense Colonel William Dudley. Dudley's unit sprinted ahead and soon arrived at the location. With 800 troops under his command, he landed boats on the northern bank of the Maumee to storm the British batteries. Dudley's men fought multiple engagements on both sides of the river before disabling the British cannons using ramrods. With things seeming to turn in the Americans' favor, a new development arose. Dudley's men began taking surprise fire from farther afield, within the dense woods of the Ohio wilderness. Although plans called for the Kentuckians to enter Fort Meigs, Dudley soon lost control of his men. They ignored his orders to head for the fort and instead pursued the second enemy. Tecumseh, famed Shawnee leader, lay in wait in the dense forest with a large band of his warriors. And just when the Kentuckians were about to attain victory against the British forces, Natives shot salvos at them. It was an invitation to yet another fight, one the Kentuckians could not resist.

It was at precisely this moment that local folklore explains the panicked flailing of our ghost soldier. From his vantage point, he knew of the trap being set by fierce Shawnee warriors hidden in the woods. Harrison's troops knew of the Shawnees' skills in guerrilla warfare. As increasing numbers of Dudley's men drew deeper into the forest, the fort's guns could no longer reach them to provide cover. Perhaps it was the fog of war and the exhilaration of spiking the British guns that led to an overconfidence in Dudley's men. In any case, our ghost soldier's desperate pleas for the impassioned men to halt could not stop the carnage to come.

In a final act of futility, Colonel Dudley followed his disobedient troops farther into the trees. Of the 800 total troops at the start, only 150 survived

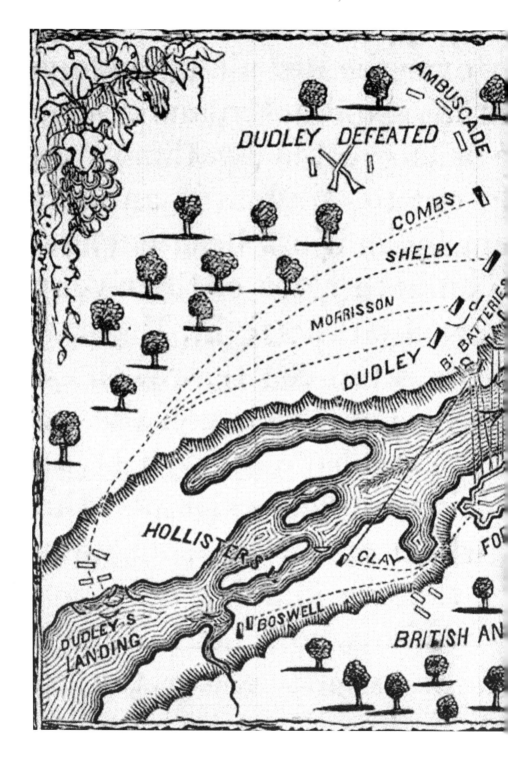

Map of Siege of Fort
Meigs from the *Pictorial
Field Book of the War
of 1812*. Benson John
Lossing, author-illustrator.
Public domain.

and eventually found their way to the safety of Fort Meigs. Colonel William Dudley was not one of them. He fell in the woods alongside the vast majority of his men. This saga would come to be known as Dudley's Massacre. Although the unit was decimated, the remainder of General Clay's force later arrived at Fort Meigs, finally offering Harrison's men the reprieve they so desperately needed.

DEATH NO STRANGER

This dramatic story offers a painful lesson about the needless slaughter of American soldiers to their own hubris. Remarkably, this was not the first time Fort Meigs had confronted death on a massive scale. In fact, from the time of its inception, this place was tied to hunger, strife, disease and misery. All of these elements prove fertile ground for folklore to spring forth, as it has for centuries.

Consider the conditions under which the fort was built during the bitter winter days of February 1813. The trees had to be cleared by hand. When the ground wasn't frozen solid, it was thick with mud, sometimes so deep a man sunk in to his knees. Constructing a fort on a riverbank within the Great Black Swamp proved a miserable feat. This forlorn section of land had long repelled pioneering settlers and military forces alike. Wagon wheels sank deep in its ever-soaking mud. Traversing the wilds proved almost impossible for most. This is what made the natural waterways like the Maumee River such a critical means of transport.

On first arriving at the site in freezing temperatures, Harrison's men worked sunup to sundown felling trees by hand, then dragging them to the site. Wood was plentiful, as native forest surrounded them on all sides. Food supplies, however, were limited. At night, weary men retreated to their tents and started small fires. Soldiers boiled corn, hominy and whatever meager rations were available to them. Most men fell into an exhausted, shivering sleep before rising the next morning to frigid winds blowing off the surface of the river. Even after the outer perimeter of the fort was completed, work remained. There were trenches to dig and blockhouses to be constructed. The hardships were never-ending.

Records gathered from soldiers' personal accounts suggest that the winter of 1813 was unusually severe for the region. One sentinel froze to death after remaining at his post for less than two hours. Untold numbers of men succumbed to mumps, measles, whooping cough and other distempers.

Many of these ailments would have been successfully treated had these unfortunate men not been on the frontier, too far from most medical interventions available at the time. Men died daily, without the warmth and comfort of a loving family member to give them a heartfelt goodbye. As the number of the dead mounted, so did the feelings of despair in the hearts of those who remained.

When the siege finally commenced three months later, Harrison's troops were already accustomed to frequent fire from the British at Fort Miamis downriver and from Native forces stalking in the trees. These Shawnee warriors fired on them incessantly. The balls from their rifles sometimes fell harmless to the ground. But on occasion, they found their mark, causing fatal wounds.

The most dangerous position during the siege was covering the magazine, which was stored in a small blockhouse. Once the British realized its location within the fort, much of their gunfire was directed there in hopes of causing a catastrophic explosion. Once, a shell landed on the blockhouse's roof, falling through it and lodging in one of the braces. It spun and smoldered there, just feet above the magazine, as nearby panic-stricken soldiers awaited certain death. Remarkably, one soldier gathered the courage to grab a boat hook and pull the hissing bomb to dry ground.

One recorded story of a man who lost his life in the siege is that of Captain Jack Shore. A former sailor, he was a private among General Harrison's troops. Perhaps he should have stayed at sea, considering the terrible end he met fighting on the ground. When the siege began, he held firm at his station at one of the fort's principal batteries. He was a master at handling the cannons, until one cannon dismounted from a direct shot, causing an iron splinter to pierce his leg. The wound was superficial and easily enough bandaged. But a few hours later, a searing pain grew unbearable for the poor sailor. The swift diagnosis was the dreaded lockjaw, known today as tetanus. Captain Shore suffered painful muscle contractions resulting in his eventual inability to breathe. Those around him helplessly watched his slow, grueling death.

Many men died lengthy and agonizing deaths, most from standard battle wounds for which there was no doctor to treat them. Few lifesaving measures were available. The lucky ones who survived earned the great "fortune" of watching others around them die. Some survivors took to reading Bible passages aloud to their expiring comrades. What more could they do? They read on through heartbreaking cries, desperate pleas and calls for distant loved ones. Finally, a silence rested over the tortured souls, ushering them into eternity.

Most of the fallen were buried somewhere nearby, some on the banks of the Maumee, others in unmarked graves just outside the fort's walls. Others were buried within the fort itself. During the most active part of the siege, leaving the refuge of the fort for any reason, even to bury the dead, was a suicide mission.

A SIEGE ENDED

Two days after the slaughter of Americans known as Dudley's Massacre, the conflict surprisingly diminished. Further attempts to breach the fort had proven futile, a reality that soon discouraged British and Native forces alike. On May 7, terms were drawn to allow for the exchange of prisoners. Although small skirmishes continued, by May 9, British leadership had abandoned the siege altogether. With the withdrawal of British forces, the Americans claimed victory. Preceding this bloody siege was a series of disastrous American defeats at historic locations like Fort Mackinac, Fort Dearborn and Fort Detroit. By holding the fort here, at this remote post along the Maumee River, the United States demonstrated its resolve as a young but tenacious republic.

The tide of the war had turned.

Shortly after the battle at Fort Meigs, British forces attempted to storm Fort Stephenson, near present-day Fremont, Ohio. They were defeated, taking serious casualties. September 1813 saw the start of the Battle of Lake Erie, an epic maritime conflagration that displayed the superiority of the U.S. Navy. This cemented America's control of the lake and forced British forces to fall back to Fort Detroit.

The war would go on for another year and a half until the signing of the Treaty of Ghent in February 1815. Most scholars today consider the outcome of the war a draw, as no boundaries changed. Many agree, however, that the group that bore the greatest loss was the Native Americans. This can be said not only of the War of 1812 but nearly all dealings between Natives and white settlers of that era.

IN CONCLUSION

Although once the site of much disease, death and misery, the Fort Meigs of today is a treasured location to residents within and beyond Wood

County's borders. It's a bustling center of cultural events, including annual reenactments of battle scenes. Visitors can also try their hand at needlework and blacksmithing, hearthside cooking, miniature war games and crossbow and other weapon demonstrations.

Of these events, among the most popular are the yearly ghost walks held during Halloween season. The draw these tours have for so many reflects a fascination with the alleged spirits who remain there. The fort's remarkable role in our young nation's history may be what initially attracts many newcomers to the place. But its reputation as a holding place for lost souls, soldiers still fighting to defend our young nation, holds a growing allure.

At a time when this spot was considered a remote and untamed wilderness, a small band of soldiers broke frozen ground and proclaimed it U.S. territory. Thinking little to nothing of the Native peoples who'd already lived here for centuries, they confronted freezing temperatures, infectious disease and enemies on all sides. Despite the odds, they held firm. Those who didn't succumb to enemy fire or wretched disease were left to bury those who did. As a result, a country in its infancy took its first steps forward, consummating its sovereignty.

America has certainly grown since those early days, in some ways virtuous and in others vile. As this unique experiment carries forward, what's most vital is a recollection of the past and the lessons it contains. If spirits do remain at this storied location, perhaps they mean to tell us of the misery of war, the impact of expansion and the struggles to survive in a new frontier.

4

THE LEGEND OF HOLCOMB ROAD

Long before haunted houses existed, haunted woods circled the globe. Homer knew it. The Brothers Grimm knew it. In legend, all the great mythic quests of self-discovery begin with the hero entering a dark wood.
—Robert Dunbar

In the flattened landscape that is Northwest Ohio, dense patches of forest are scattered among vast fields of grain. They represent a small slice of what the topography of this region once was: an untamed swamp, overrun with maple, sycamore and oak trees. Centuries after early pioneers' plowshares first gripped the soil, wooded sections are left standing in neat plots. From above, these impenetrable woods take on geometric dimensions. They stand as dark-green squares and rectangles against a muted canvas of farmland.

Crops tend to be planted along highways and county roads, allowing farmers easy access to their fields. Native woods that remain today are usually located away from any roads. But in a few instances, a wooded section runs right up alongside a road. This is especially true around winding creeks and streams that require vegetation along their banks to prevent erosion.

Trees running along both sides of a roadway is a rarity in these parts. This is especially true for old-growth forests, with tall trees that hoover and sway, casting forlorn county roads into darkness. In these locations, a kind of ancient wilderness engulfs unsuspecting motorists. For most people born and raised in the area, getting to the woods requires some planning and hiking. The woods don't come unbidden. Normally.

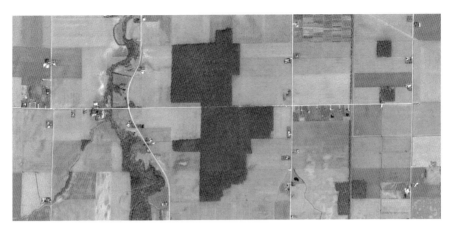

Satellite view of Holcomb Woods on Holcomb Road. *Google Maps, imagery ©2022, Maxar Technologies, State of Ohio, OSIP, USDA/FPAC/GEO.*

Common county road along a waterway with wooded section running along one side.

Entrance into Holcomb Woods, facing east, September 2022.

Perhaps that explains the decades-long fascination with one Wood County road known as Holcomb.

Located about ten miles east of Bowling Green, Holcomb Road is a nondescript paved road just a little over four miles in length. It crosses the south branch of the Portage River next to the Church of the Good Shepherd. Perhaps a couple dozen homes and farms claim an address on the

Entrance into Holcomb Woods, facing west, September 2022.

fabled stretch. These mundane traits belie the road's role in local legend. For decades, wonder seekers have journeyed to this spot, where a canopy of trees holds thick overhead, shrouding the ground below. The shaded length of this road runs only about three-tenths of a mile. While that's short in length, this dark space runs deep in the imaginations of many.

A TALE FOR THE AGES

As with many urban legends, a narrative has congealed over time as to the significance of this foreboding place. It's been shared over campfires, games of cornhole and craft brews purchased at local bars. The story has gained so much notoriety that it's now the subject of a feature-length film, *The Legend of Holcomb Road*.

When the picture was released in 2018, it sold out early screenings. Director Matt Erman of Fostoria states it is his best-performing film. Made entirely with locals, the movie portrays the folktale as it has come to be

Movie poster of *The Legend of Holcomb Road*. The film was released in 2018. *Graphic: Matt Erman, director.*

known through oral storytelling. As of this writing, this movie is available for streaming on Amazon's platform.

The legend is usually told as some variation of the following. There once was a school bus full of children driven by a crazed and angry man. It's said he'd gone mad because of the unruly children on his route. His nerves were frayed, leaving him vulnerable to wild impulses. On entering the dark and obstructed section of the road, the driver sped the bus off the shoulder. It plowed over a few small saplings before hitting a hefty oak. The driver flew through the windshield and collided with the trunk. His lifeless body laid among the wreckage as flames ignited, spreading quickly through the bus. Children wailed as they tried to open jammed doors and windows, some breaking out cracked glass with their fists. A few made their way out. Others succumbed to the heavy smoke building inside.

It's said that in order to trigger a ghostly experience at the spot, drivers must head down Holcomb Road from Highway 199 toward the edge of the woods. On making a U-turn to face the highway, they will lose radio and cellphone signals. And at night, on completing this ritual and turning off the headlights, a single sphere of light will appear hovering over the road at a distance. In moments, those who can stand the tension will see the light speeding toward them, growing in size and brightness until it reaches them, disappearing as it veers off the shoulder into nearby trees.

It's also said that the tree that bore the impact of the bus still stands. Reportedly, an uncanny image of the driver's face can be seen in its bark. Many have also claimed to hear the disembodied screams of dying children emanating from the darkened trees.

Separating Fiction from Fact

Despite the longevity of this folktale, no known records exist as to a fatal bus crash. It would have been a tragedy of epic proportions, considering the tale's claim that innocent—if unruly—children perished in the flames. So how did this story come to exist?

Many locals recall having seen a disabled bus parked at the edge of the woods for many years in the 1970s. Apparently, the property owner at that time collected scrap metal and left an aged bus rotting there. It must have been quite the juxtaposition: a school bus, the symbol of childhood for so many, parked at the entrance to an ominous and shadowy place. The stark scene called for an explanation. And in the collective imaginations of so

Section from center of Holcomb Road showing graffiti, September 2022.

many Wood County residents, a story began to come together, one that remains common knowledge among those living in the area today.

It's important to consider that although this section of Holcomb Road is often visited by wonder seekers, it remains private property. Anyone venturing off the public thoroughfare is trespassing. It's important to respect the rights of the living, whatever readers may believe on the existence of the dead. Clearly, many visitors have chosen to leave their mark on the road itself.

LESSONS LEARNED

This place has had a draw for so many for so long. Some come seeking ghostly encounters. Some are enticed by the natural beauty of the spot. And some, unfortunately, come in despair. A case in point is that of Jerald Rose. He was a BGSU senior in 1975. On October 25 of that year, a motorist passing on Holcomb Road spotted Rose's idling car on the shoulder. A hose was taped and sealed to the tailpipe and threaded through a crack in one of the passenger windows. Soon, the sheriff's office was contacted, and the coroner was summoned. The Clyde native was pronounced dead as a result of suicide by carbon monoxide poisoning. No note was left explaining the tragedy.

We're left guessing at what desperation led to the act. It's possible that the location's legendary reputation brought Rose there. Whatever the case, it is one Holcomb Road death that *is* found in the historical record. Of course, any death is one too many. If you or someone you know is considering suicide, there is help. The National Suicide Prevention Hotline can be reached by dialing or texting 988 from anywhere in the United States.

For the vast majority of those who sojourn there, Holcomb Road is a place of wonder and fascination. It's unexpected places like this that so often entice us. They bring attention to the world beyond us. They awaken us from our routine lives. They ignite a collective storytelling that allows us to explore our vulnerabilities and confront our mortality.

That is what the legend of Holcomb Road still offers us today.

5

INDIAN HILLS

ROSSFORD'S NATIVE HERITAGE

The voice of the Great Spirit is heard in the twittering of birds,
the rippling of mighty waters and the sweet breathing of flowers.
—Zitkala-Sa

Not far from the southern bank of the Maumee, past the glitz and opulence of the Hollywood Casino, stands an odd structure nestled at the edge of a dense wood. More than fifty years old, this building of modern design contrasts starkly with the ancient forest that surrounds it. Sided in dark-brown sheet metal with sharp geometric features, one might assume it is some New Age science lab or perhaps a manufacturing facility for the production of technological devices. It is, of course, neither of these.

Indian Hills Elementary School opened to Rossford students in 1970. The district raised $1.4 million for its construction. It was the first new elementary school built in the district since 1929. Wanting to make the most of the new facility, designers included fourteen classrooms along with a gymnasium and cafeteria. It was to be one of the district's crowning achievements to date. Perhaps the ultramodern design aimed to capture that sentiment. Here, students would grow their minds in a facility that, from the looks of it, could have just as easily housed NASA's revered Apollo program.

Top: View of shuttered Indian Hills Elementary School, September 2022.

Bottom: Satellite view of woods surrounding Indian Hills Elementary. *Google Maps, imagery ©2022, Maxar Technologies, State of Ohio, OSIP, USDA/FPAC/GEO.*

For all the focus on the purpose and functionality of the new building, one very different aspect has become better understood over time. It has nothing to do with the building itself, as notable as it is to anyone driving past 401 Glenwood Road. What is most remarkable about this unusual location has to do with the land on which it sits, including the dense woods surrounding the shuttered school. A string of historical discoveries decades in the making, coupled with a wide collection of odd spiritual experiences at the site, point to a significance that wasn't fully grasped when the school was built half a century ago.

Native Spirits

Indian Hills Elementary School was permanently closed by the Rossford school district in 2015. For more than four decades, it served as many youngsters' first school experience. It was here that kids began to read and discovered the unrivaled joy of recess. Such can be said of elementary schools anywhere. But what's unique about this spot requires some explaining. Let's start with the ever-growing accumulation of mysterious occurrences at the location. Former students, staff, visitors and passersby have reported strange happenings during the life span of the school.

One of the most common claims includes the disembodied rhythmic pounding of faint but distinct drums emanating from the surrounding woods. Listening carefully on the darkest of nights, one can often hear the iconic pulsing beat. At once eerie and ephemeral, it evokes a kind of connection with an ancient culture that once inhabited this space. At least, that's the general consensus of those lucky enough to have heard it. For the many children who heard it over the years, the drums became a kind of siren call, a test of courage. On hearing it, a middle-schooler would turn to his buddy and issue the challenge, "Wanna go see where it's coming from?"

On weekdays, after school was over, latchkey kids bent on proving their mettle joined hide-and-seek games being held among the trees in the dark woods beyond the school's perimeters.

Some who've lived near the school, on neighborhood streets like Marilyn Drive, Carol Circle and Oak Street, have reported growing up in haunted homes. Classic accounts of phantom footsteps, unexpected cold spots and faint moans have been reported in these houses. What's most curious, however, are the few reports of full-bodied apparitions clad in centuries-old Native attire.

Regarding accounts that come from the school building itself, former staff have claimed that various items went missing, only to show up in the oddest of places, like a stapler missing from a teacher's desk drawer, later found on top of a tall storage cabinet. Such occurrences could easily be explained as pranks by mischievous students. Harder to explain is the account of a custodian who, late at night, having just finished vacuuming and shutting off the sweeper, heard a startling crash ring out from the kitchen area of the cafeteria. The custodian, believing he'd been alone in the building, sprinted in the direction of the clatter. On arriving, he found every pot and pan that had been suspended from the ceiling on J-hooks scattered on the floor.

Gymnasium inside closed Indian Hills Elementary School, September 2022.

This is to say nothing of multiple sightings of ghostly figures in the building itself over the years. Inside the gymnasium, a frequent foreboding feeling is often noted, including the stench of something burning. Dave Misko and Brian Dreier-Morgan of the Paranormal Mysteries team investigated there in November 2021. They documented personal accounts of the building's unexplained activities by interviewing former staff members. They also captured disembodied electronic voice phenomena (EVPs), including what sounded like a growl. The team's electromagnetic field meters (EMFs) detected unusual amounts of electromagnetic activity in the proximity of the building's grounds.

GHOSTLY TROPE, CONFIRMED

Claims of paranormal activity sprouting forth from Native burial grounds are the basis of countless folktales across the country. A premise this trite is sure to prove false, right?

Rossford native Nancy Stonerock recalls one chilly Saturday morning in December 1959. At the time, she was the den mother for her young sons' Cub Scout troop. On a quest to earn merit badges, she directed the group on a hike into what was then known as Crane's Woods. It would be more than ten years before ground was broken for the construction of Indian Hills Elementary. Back then, the whole acreage was a wild section of swampy forest.

Nancy's father once told her that this section of woods was rumored to have been a Native burial ground. She could not recall how her father came to know this, other than to say that it was an accepted fact among residents at large. When her Cub Scouts needed to earn a nature-based hiking badge, the location seemed the perfect fit for the task. The going was slow at points, due to the wet and muddy conditions of the trail. But the boys seemed invigorated by the intriguing historical claim. When the effort was finished, they vowed to return in warmer months to continue searching for evidence that confirmed the rumors.

By May 1961, the boys' persistence, fueled by the childlike wonder that springs eternal, paid off. Like the plot of a great kid movie, this group of youngsters made a discovery that had so long eluded adults. Their success was chronicled in the May 23, 1961 edition of the *Findlay Republican Courier.*

> *Scouts Discover Indian Grave in Rossford Area—Bowling Green (AP)— Graves identified as those of Indians, possibly Ottawas, were uncovered Saturday by members of a Rossford Boy Scout troop. The find, including two skulls, reasonably well-preserved, and other bones were made on a bluff about 40 feet above Grassy Creek, near Rossford. Lyle Fletcher, assistant professor of geography at Bowling Green State University, who has an interest in Indian lore, said they were probably of Ottawas, who ranged this area until after the turn of the 19th century. Fletcher estimated they were 200 to 300 years old. The scouts found no artifacts such as arrowheads or pottery. Further digging at the site was suspended pending possible future exploration.*

In the years that followed, a fervor to find more evidence of Native burials only grew. The common lore passed down from one generation of Rossford locals to the next had now been verified. This led many locals to essentially loot the site for souvenirs. Whatever was easily spotted on the surface of the ground was soon taken. Although some cursory efforts to preserve the site were made by academic researchers in the following years, it was too late. There simply wasn't much left to protect in terms of what was visible on the ground.

By late June 1967, the site had caught the interest of Earl Prahl, instructor of anthropology at the University of Toledo. An archaeological dig began under his direction. It was to be the first professional excavation ever conducted in Northwest Ohio. One of its first discoveries was a common grave of "bundle" burials holding the remains of twenty Native American individuals. The bones contained therein were removed and taken to laboratories at UT for further study. Newspaper accounts from August 1968 state that by then, the team had recovered the remains of thirty-five Native individuals. All remains were being kept in a repository at UT. It was hoped that further investigation would reveal their sex, age, physical development, diseases and causes of death.

Photo taken from within a dense wooded section showing the edge of one of the burial mounds, September 2022.

Excavations continued in the summers of 1967 and 1968. No attempts were made to reach out to descendants of these ancient Native peoples. It's a glaring omission by today's standards. For reasons explained later in this chapter, the exclusion of Native voices in how the excavations were handled has had lasting effects. It's an insult and a disgrace toward an entire group of our fellow citizens. It also remains an issue for how this location may be utilized in the future.

The archaeological team of the late 1960s consisted of professional, student and amateur archaeologists alike. Digs were located adjacent to the Harris railroad yards and extended along the banks of Grassy Creek. Although initially attributed to Woodland tribes like the Ottawa, it soon became apparent that this burial ground originated hundreds of years earlier. Artifacts and remains collected from these digs pointed to a time before Europeans settled the region. Discovered items aligned with artifacts from other digs of ancient settlements along the southern shore of Lake Erie and contiguous areas of Michigan.

At its completion, the excavation revealed the footprint of a Native village complete with defensive fortifications, circular residential structures and ossuaries. Evidence was found of at least two separate occupations, one around AD 1000 and the other about AD 1500. A stockade of saplings had surrounded the village, offering some protection from attack from other tribes. The imprint of fortifications in three parallel rows one thousand feet long were found along Grassy Creek. While discovering these perimeters, the team unearthed other items, including projectile points, pottery shards, polished stone axe heads known as celts, pipe fragments and large numbers of fish and mammal bones. This kind of refuse offered insight as to the diet of those who once lived there.

The burials themselves were unique compared to those found in excavations conducted along Erie's shores. Here, bones were found in bundles assembled long after death, not as whole skeletons in individual graves. Each individual's remains were cleaned and bundled together. In most cases, these bundles were buried with others in a large pit. No evidence of violence or mutilation was found, suggesting that this was a common funereal practice. This may reflect a spiritual belief that tribal connections persisted beyond death. There may have been a ceremony every year, when fresh individual graves were exhumed in order to place descendants' remains in a communal grave. Similar mass burials discovered in Central Ohio date back as far as 2,300 years. Communal graves suggest that these tribes held spiritual beliefs around a shared afterlife.

Inexplicably, the solitary skull of a child was found among a pile of refuse outside the fortified walls of the village. Newspaper articles reported that the archaeological team carefully cataloged the locations of items found at the site and then transported the pieces for storage on UT's campus. A computer was used to study how the items were dispersed in the hopes that more could be understood about how the village operated. At the time of these efforts in the late 1960s, little was known about Native settlements prior to the arrival of Europeans.

A School Built on Hallowed Grounds

Even before the archaeological digs began in the summer of 1968, in March of that year, Superintendent Wayne Hosafros announced the name of what would become Rossford's newest school. In honor of the initial discoveries made by Rossford Boy Scouts in 1961, the school would be called Indian Hills Elementary. Completion of construction was set for August 1969, allowing a full year to prepare the building to accept students the following fall. Furthermore, Superintendent Hosafros declared that a large display case in the school's front lobby would house artifacts taken from the wooded thirty-nine-acre lot.

That display case, featured so prominently at the school's main entrance, became part of the school's identity, distinguishing it from other schools. Former students recall being encouraged by staff to search for more artifacts for inclusion in the case. It was a kind of treasure hunt for students venturing into the woods. They weren't looking for ghostly experiences. Instead, they sought the tangible remains of an ancient people. Some students found items such as whole human bones and bone fragments, as well as shards of pottery. Students were rewarded with a piece of candy when they brought their finds to the school office. It's said that artifacts were once quite easy to find, especially in an open field in the middle of the woods.

Unbelievably, priceless artifacts became lost in what amounted to a child's game. What became of this display case and its contents is unknown. It's hard to understand the glibness with which adults in positions of authority viewed the tangible remains of our Native heritage.

In the years following the school's opening, smaller digs continued under the direction of Earl Prahl. Additional discoveries included three-foot, fire-blackened circles—the remains of campfires. One fire pit included human bone fragments, an indication that some bodies had been cremated. This funereal practice differed from the bundle burials found elsewhere on the site and indicated that the location may have been used by different tribal groups spanning several centuries. In addition, the skeletons of birds and fish no longer local to the region were discovered. Artifacts removed during these digs were housed in UT's sociology-anthropology building.

Archaeological digs of various sites across the state grew in number in subsequent years. Some were in Northwest Ohio, including a site on the Maumee River in Waterville. Examples from Southwest Ohio included burial mounds discovered in Dayton and Mason. As more ancient sites were revealed, many people grew concerned about the need to preserve Native cultural heritage. But these locations were subject to pressure from land developers. In response, the Ohio Historical Connection set up a registry of Indian mounds, earthworks and settlement sites. The collection of artifacts and human remains without a permit on State or Federal property in Ohio was prohibited. Unfortunately, today there are virtually no regulations protecting most sites on private land in Ohio. State statute ORC 149.54 requires archaeologists conducting surveys to maintain a minimum of training and education. Private citizens can excavate suspected Native sites on their own property without State oversight or regulation.

Today, when ancestral Native remains are inadvertently discovered on State property, the Ohio Historic Preservation Office maintains standardized procedures for preserving the site and its cultural heritage. Within seventy-two hours of confirming Native provenance of the items discovered, affected tribes are consulted. A plan of action for the site is created in collaboration with tribal descendants. Together, they set a course for the "treatment, handling, custodianship, curation, and disposition of the American Indian ancestral remains and cultural items discovered" (Ohio History Connection, American Indian Policy Statement).

Indian Hills of Today and Tomorrow

On September 20, 1979, the Indian Hills site was officially listed in the National Register of Historic Places for the State of Ohio. It's a known ancestral aboriginal village and includes burial sites. Successive archaeological digs from the late 1960s to the early 1980s revealed the site's unprecedented significance as a connection between historic and prehistoric peoples of the area. The protohistoric tribe known as the Assistaeronon (Nation of Fire) was an Algonquian-speaking ethnic group whose membership stretched along Lake Erie's western shore and into Canada as far as the Niagara Peninsula.

For as much historical significance as the Indian Hills site holds, for all the fascination it has drawn from local residents over the years, questions remain as to its role in the community moving forward. In early 2022, Rossford City Council sought public input on what might be done with the property. Indian Hills Elementary was permanently closed in 2015. Since then, the building and the thirty-nine-acre lot on which it stands has been unused. Todd Audet, Rossford's director of economic development, headed up the investigation on whether the site met requirements under the National Historic Preservation Act 106 program. Additional digs were planned to determine whether sections of the lot containing no artifacts could be split off and developed. The city pledged to work with the State Historic Preservation Office (SHPO) to determine the best path forward. Some residents suggested using the space for affordable housing, including a senior living community. Others liked the idea of a park to expand green space within the city.

Surveyors broke ground on the project in April 2022. A ten-acre section on the eastern side of the whole thirty-nine-acre parcel had already been identified as the site of the Native village and burial grounds. The city took a deliberate and careful approach in considering what steps to take. It would ensure that new development was not occurring on historically significant grounds. In perhaps a nod to mistakes from decades past, when the site was robbed of artifacts in plain sight, the city now sought to preserve what remained of the Native village and burial grounds in coordination with SHPO.

The investigation covered the thirteen-acre section on the other side of the lot, where the school building still stands. From that effort, only one projectile point was discovered, under a leaf on top of the ground, of all things. Systematic shovel surveys of the section proposed for development showed no artifacts of archaeological significance. The results of the survey were sent to the SHPO. The city then asked that the thirteen-acre section be removed from restrictions on development that would still apply to the remaining acreage. The city also expressed interest in following the same process with another, eight-acre section as well.

Native tribes associated with the site also have input in any plans. Some experts have placed Indian Hills' significance on par with the Serpent Mound and Newark Earthworks sites in Ohio. Some have suggested designating the Indian Hills site as a historical park, comparable to the aforementioned sites. Others, including some representatives of Native tribes, feel it should be left alone, as is. When the research on the property is completed, a master map of the area will be made indicating the remaining areas of preservation restrictions.

In the meantime, the locations of artifacts removed from decades-old digs have been determined. Some artifacts were sent to the Cleveland Museum of Natural History. Human remains were transferred from the University of Toledo to Firelands Archaeology, a nonprofit organization. In 2021, these remains were sent to the Ohio History Connection in Columbus for permanent curation.

The mishandling of Native remains and artifacts among university and museum systems at large was recently revealed as a prevalent nationwide phenomenon. A September 15, 2022 article in the *New York Times* detailed a controversial case at the University of North Dakota. And in April 2023, the Indian Affairs Committee of the U.S. Senate convened a hearing on the Native American Graves Protection and Repatriation Act (NAGPRA). They named the Ohio History Connection among five organizations as "unacceptable" in their retention of ancestral remains and objects. The committee pressed any organization that knowingly keeps sacred objects to return them to their rightful owners, the descendant members of these Native tribes. A ProPublica investigation, also from April 2023, revealed that the Ohio History Connection retains at least 7,100 Native remains in its custody, making it the second-largest collection of unrepatriated Native American remains in the country. Only the University of California, Berkeley, holds a larger collection.

E Pluribus Unum

Sometimes a good story, told time and again over generations, evolves into common knowledge. Like a badge, we wear the "truths" of our people proudly. These elements of the place we're from make up our collective identity. To be from Rossford, from Wood County, from Northwest Ohio, means that this story is part and parcel of who we are.

Through the years, many have doubted the supernatural claims of this place. Some still do, of course. Others, like those who felt the distant drumming reverberating in their chest, those who discovered an arrowhead poking out from deadened leaves, those who glimpsed the misty figure of a warrior from centuries ago, know that something of substance remains from this ancient past.

One of the most remarkable findings from researchers in the 1960s was the unusual bundle burials found at the site. From this, researchers theorized that an archaic tribe of Assistaeronon people believed in an afterlife in which all are reunited with the tribe. Reinterment in mass graves helped ensure that each individual remained a member of the wider community. Out of many, one. This focus on connection and interdependence is a message worth noting today. Most of us spend much of our days in front of screens instead of engaging with those around us. This practice grants the illusion that we don't really need one another.

It seems the spirits of Indian Hills know otherwise. We would be wise to heed their advice.

6

HAUNTED SOUTH MAIN SCHOOL

Old buildings whisper to us in the creaking of floorboards
and the rattling of windowpanes.
—*Fennel Hudson*

Many schools built in the late nineteenth century haven't survived the wrecking ball. Most school districts elected to tear them down to build new facilities in order to accommodate the growing numbers of students. Crumbling walls, tired boiler furnaces and deteriorating classrooms were just too costly to maintain. The few antiquated school buildings that remained were left with quiet hallways and paint-chipped walls. Such is true for the stately brick edifice at 437 South Main Street in Bowling Green, Ohio. Remarkably, it still stands today.

South Main School first opened its doors in 1890, at a time in our history when American football was first played at the collegiate level and the automobile was about to replace horse-driven carts. Until that time, education in Ohio was largely limited to one-room schoolhouses. These quaint structures still dot the landscape today. But at the turn of the twentieth century, public education was moving toward a new model of instruction, toward the teaching of children in graduated levels according to their ages and abilities. This required larger facilities with separate classrooms for each grade.

Bowling Green has long been known for valuing education. This college town hosts the venerable Bowling Green State University, a storied state

Front façade of South Main School at 437 South Main Street, Bowling Green, Ohio, September 2022.

institution that serves about 20,000 students every year. Way back in 1890, only about 3,500 residents lived in the community. The university wouldn't be founded for another twenty years. It seems the small village's focus on education grew into the lasting influence that persists today.

South Main School welcomed students for 115 years until its closing in 2005. After the school closed, the Bowling Green community began making new uses of the building. This included the creation of a dojo, the formation of a common space for the arts and the establishment of a day care for children. The three-story building then became dormant after a period

A classroom on the first floor of South Main School, July 2022.

of years. Many locals drove by the place countless times, thinking nothing of it. For others, however, unusual experiences planted seeds of folktales that are still growing today. Stairwells that once echoed with noisy children have fallen silent. Playground equipment has rusted in the shadow of the lonesome structure. Perhaps this decay allowed spirits to take firm residence of the place. Perhaps empty classrooms felt welcoming to lost souls. By all signs, these spirits grew bold and unafraid to make their presence known. If it's true that ghosts prefer old, abandoned structures to eke out their existences, South Main School is the perfect place to roam free from the intrusions of the living.

Perhaps class is still in session.

But just who are these lost souls? Why might they have chosen South Main School as their eternal resting place? There's a presumption that spirits remain forever stuck at the location of their death. According to records, however, no children ever lost their lives in the school. What then might account for claims of child spirits? What story might explain the presence of ghosts roaming the halls and classrooms? Amazingly, historical research unearths a compelling story of one former student and his adventurous, if reckless, ways.

THE LIFE AND TIMES OF LESTER MCCOOL

Lester McCool was born in 1888, just two years before South Main School opened its doors. He was the third son of Jacob and Mary McCool, a growing family in Scrubgrass, Pennsylvania. The couple added two more sons and a daughter before making the move to Bowling Green, Ohio. Jacob found work as a pumper in the oil fields that dotted Wood County. The family settled into a house at the corner of Grove and Pearl Streets, a four-block walk from the school. Lester and his five siblings were among the first students to occupy the new building. No doubt, living nearby meant a quick commute, especially welcome when the winter winds blew.

We don't everything about Lester, but we do know a lot about his character and reputation in the community. That's due to the manner of his death. Stories about it appeared in local newspapers for days. He had been known as "the most popular and most exemplary young man in the city, and his untimely death was universally mourned," according to the *Wood County Sentinel* of July 30, 1908.

The tragedy of that singular moment shocked the small community and set it buzzing. Townspeople whispered to one another regarding what actually happened to poor Lester, the young man known for his active role at the local Young Men's Christian Association (better known today as the YMCA).

Lester had struggled throughout his schooling, and at age twenty, he was about to graduate from high school. The plan had been for him to finish his senior year the following spring. Knowing this, he and two of his closest friends, Howard Decker and Russell Bates, vowed to set off on the adventure of their young lives—a "lark," as Howard preferred to call it. The young men knew a life of hard work and toil awaited them after graduating. But that chapter hadn't quite arrived. Before them stretched the glorious summer of 1908—the summer before their senior year.

They would go as far as the fates would carry them, westward. Tales of Lewis and Clark from elementary school history lessons echoed in their minds as the threesome started an exploration of their own making. For the first leg of the journey, they scrounged what spare cash they had to purchase train tickets for as far west as the money would allow. That turned out to be Kansas.

Kansas it was.

They decided to figure out the rest when they got there. They'd find work where they could. The world stretched far beyond Northwest Ohio. They were about to seize it for themselves.

The story, as I'm relaying it to you, comes through Howard's telling. Russell chickened out shortly after the journey began. Or perhaps you could say he came to his senses. Either way, he stepped off the train at one of the numerous stops along the way. Perhaps he apologized to Lester and Howard, wringing his hat, excusing himself on account of some sweetheart who begged him to stay home. Whatever the reason, the threesome was reduced to a pair. Lester and Howard would carry on.

Soon their train pulled into Monument, Kansas. Just picture them, bursting out of the passenger car, the steam engine spewing white-hot plumes as their eager feet glided across the platform of the station. According to Howard, they immediately took to canvassing the entire town, a process that took just minutes. Even today, this tiny town is unincorporated. No one had explained to the young men that Monument was simply a train stop and a small collection of houses that supported the rail workers. There was nothing to see or do.

It's not hard to imagine the disappointment that must have sunk deep in their chests. Their friend had lost heart and turned home, and the first stop on their grand adventure turned out to be nothing but a few rickety shacks alongside a train station, all of which was surrounded by endless fields of grain.

Just what were they to do now, and with empty pockets no less?

As Howard later told reporters, they had no other option than to set off on foot. They hoped to happen upon some bustling hamlet and, most important, opportunities for work. They made it as far as Page City, another unincorporated speck of a town. The sun was setting as they approached the outskirts. In truth, they were both fighting exhaustion by that time, and the discouragement in their hearts was a heavy load to carry. They planned to stop and sleep under the stars. Then, after a good rest, they'd set out again, moving westward, toward whatever destiny had in store.

The next morning, they heard from a resident that a town called Winona was only six miles down Highway 40. Their spirits lifted, and a bounce returned to their steps. They could cover six miles easily, and with any luck, they would not have to sleep on the ground another night.

As they neared Winona, the two crawled under a small rail bridge to cool themselves in the shade. It was then that they heard the screech of a freight train in the distance across the flattened landscape. Lester popped his head up from under the bridge to get a better look. Sure enough, about five miles out, he could see the distinct white plume of the engine. It was headed toward them. In a frenzied exuberance, Lester yelled for Howard, and the two scrambled up the bank. They couldn't believe their good fortune. No more walking. No more Kansas. They'd hop this train and go as far as it would take them.

Lester was the first to attempt to board the train. Howard yelled to him, grabbing his shoulder, telling him it was moving much too fast and that they'd have to make another plan. Lester ignored his pleas. After a couple more attempts, he managed to grab hold of the rear handle of a boxcar. His grip held, but the force of the jolt threw his body into the space between the two cars, breaking his hold on the handle. The wheels from the trailing car passed over his thighs, slicing his legs clean off. Maimed, he lay alongside the tracks. Howard quickly grabbed him by the shoulders and pulled him away from the train still roaring by.

Howard untied a red kerchief from his neck and waved it desperately at the train master, who sat riding atop the caboose. The master signaled forward for the train to halt, and the brakes sounded their high-pitched squeals. The master hopped down from the caboose and ran to the two boys. He'd had the presence of mind to bring with him the stretcher that was kept for just such occasions. Transients were known to jump freighters in those days. He and Howard carried the wounded but perfectly conscious and coherent young man to the nearby train station.

On seeing his own injuries, Lester asked Howard to let him die.

The only physician in Winona was out of town. A telegraph was dispatched to nearby Oakley, from where a Dr. Winslow was dispatched. He finally arrived after an hour, but there was nothing to be done for Lester's mortal wounds. All who were present recalled the young man's alertness until he took his last breath. All were struck by his calm, his resolve and his acceptance of the inevitable. Lester blamed no one but himself.

What remained when the light drained from Lester's eyes was a traumatized and grief-stricken Howard. He was surrounded by strangers. His best friend and co-adventurer lay dead by his side. Winona's townspeople didn't know what to say or do. Eventually, a small group of women gathered wildflowers from a nearby field. They placed them on top of a casket they had procured for the unfortunate young man from Ohio.

Howard telegraphed word of the accident back home. He had to wait for money to be wired to support the return trip.

In a kind of painful irony, Howard, no doubt in a state of some shock, peacefully boarded Train 102 to accompany his friend's remains back to Bowling Green. When the train reached a stop in Fort Wayne, Indiana, the train's porter forgot to tell Howard that they had transferred the casket

BOWLING GREEN BOY

Killed by Cars in Kansas while "Jumping" a Train.

Lester, son of J. H. McCool of Bowling Green, who with Howard Deckard and Russell Bates, started about two weeks ago for the west, fell beneath a freight train at Winona, Kansas, at one o'clock Thursday afternoon and received injuries from which he died two hours later. Both legs were cut off close to the thigh. In attempting to "jump" a train he was thrown under the wheels.

The remains were brought home and funeral services were held at the McCool home at 2 o'clock Sunday afternoon. The remains were taken to Parker, Va., for interment.

Lester McCool was one of the most highly respected young men of Bowling Green, and prominently connected with Y. M. C. A. work here. He would have been a member of the graduating class of the Bowling Green High school for 1909.

Left: Article from the *Perrysburg Journal*, July 31, 1908. Newspapers.com.

Below: Rear view of South Main School, July 2022.

to another train bound for Toledo. Lester's body would arrive at its final destination without Howard. He had unknowingly missed the connection. The necessary papers, including the death certificate, were in Howard's breast pocket. This resulted in a painful delay, as the body could not be released to the family until Howard and the papers finally arrived hours later.

At first, Howard was too overcome with grief and guilt to talk to anyone of the details. Rumors began to spread around town, insinuating that foul play may have been involved. This enraged Howard and perhaps brought him out of his dissociative state. After six days of the rumors, he'd had enough. He sat down with a reporter from the *Bowling Green Sentinel-Tribune* and told the whole story.

That's why we have such rich details of the saga.

Presently, two local residents, Victoria Canterbury and her mother, Randi Canterbury, shared details as to their own haunting experiences inside the school building. Most notably, Victoria recalled once spotting the legless apparition of a young boy in period clothing. Is it possible that the maimed child spirit sometimes spotted at South Main School is the lost soul of Lester McCool, the young man who set out to explore the world and lost his life in the process? Perhaps his spirit prefers an existence that resembles a simpler time in his life, his childhood days at South Main School. Perhaps the school offers the warm memories of friends, laughter and the promise of a bright future ahead.

We'll never know for sure.

This is just one of many firsthand accounts of ghostly activity observed in the dormant, darkened building off Main Street. This reputation is common among old buildings. Something in their quiet slumber, in their crumbling façades, seems to beckon lost souls.

Fringe Paranormal Investigations

In the past, locals who wanted to learn more about South Main School could visit it. A group called Fringe Paranormal Investigations managed the property for a period of about five years, providing a range of ghost-hunting opportunities for all comers. Their website, https://hauntedsouthmainschool. wordpress.com, contains a summary of the paranormal experiences found within, including recordings of disembodied sounds and video testimonials of those with firsthand unexplained experiences. Unfortunately, the building's owner sold the structure in 2022, terminating Fringe Paranormal's lease. As of this writing, South Main School is vacant and unused.

THE LIFE AND TIMES OF PALL FORKOS

A Hungarian stonemason's body was discovered at South Main School on Sunday morning, March 28, 1909.

Pall Forkos was one of nearly 700,000 Hungarian emigrants who settled in the United States at the start of the twentieth century. One of the largest concentrations of Hungarians came to call Toledo home. You can still see remnants of their influence today. In the heart of the city, just off the southern bank of the Maumee River, stands St. Stephen's Hungarian Catholic Church. Most likely, Pall worshipped in its pews, receiving Holy Communion at Sunday morning Mass.

When it came to the workweek, Pall was as hearty a worker as you could find. Like so many of his countrymen, he had emigrated in the hopes of finding financial security and a chance to lift his family out of poverty. In 1905, at the age of thirty-seven, he embarked on a steamship out of Hamburg, Germany, leaving his wife and three children. He found work as a laborer with the Mercer Cement Block Company of Toledo, Ohio. He hoped to eventually save enough money to send for the rest of his family. He scraped together just enough funds for a deposit on a small apartment in the Hungarian neighborhood of Birmingham in burgeoning downtown Toledo.

When that fateful day in March 1909 arrived, Pall had already been working as a mason for four years. He was just short of reaching his financial goal. One extra day of work added to his weekly wage would finally put his savings over the top. He'd been dreaming every night of the day his family would arrive after their long voyage across the Atlantic. Perhaps that's why he refused to climb into the wagon at the end of the workday on Saturday, March 27, 1909. He and the rest of his crew had been putting the finishing touches on a repair to stonework at Bowling Green's South Main School. It was backbreaking work. His crewmates (mostly fellow Hungarian immigrants) were eager to return home to their community in downtown Toledo. As much as he needed the rest, Pall waved goodbye as the others climbed into the wagon. The knowledge that he'd soon see his family gave him all the energy he needed. He intended to stay all day Sunday to finish the job, earning the extra pay that would allow him to send for his wife and children. He'd spend the night on the floor of the empty school.

For all his earnest devotion to his job, Pall's deepest wish to be reunited with his family would be denied him.

In the early morning shadows, as the sun rose over Main Street, a passerby spotted the slumped figure of a man in boots and overalls. The

A view looking out of the main entrance of South Main School, July 2022.

worker hadn't made it far from the front entrance of the school. Presumably, he had overexerted himself while placing the weighty stones. Late that Saturday night, when a pain in his chest grew from an annoyance to a searing explosion, he'd dropped his tools, stumbled out onto the manicured front lawn and fell forward. There he remained until the passerby spotted his unfamiliar frame lying motionless in the cold, frosted-over grass.

A hasty examination of Pall's remains by a medical examiner concluded heart failure due to exertion. A brief notice of his tragic death was mentioned in the local newspaper and directed readers to his burial in Oak Grove Cemetery. Mysteriously, a search of burial plots in this Bowling Green cemetery found no listing for Pall Forkos. It's assumed he was placed in an unmarked grave shortly after a cursory funeral service the morning after his death. Only the undertaker and his staff were known to attend. Confoundingly, authorities stated that they were unable to notify any friends or family of his death or burial.

In the end, Pall died in the wee small hours of a Sunday morning and was buried by Monday afternoon. Why the rush? Why the lack of any real effort to notify significant others? And most important, why is his grave not recorded in cemetery records? These questions remain unanswered. It took a couple days before county officials contacted Pall's employer. His closest friends and coworkers told reporters of the years he'd spent scrimping and saving for tickets for the rest of his family to join him. Now, word of his tragic death would be received by his wife in the form of a letter, written in Hungarian and signed by his foreman. No doubt, it spoke of Pall's devotion to her and the children and of the deep sorrow the foreman felt for them all.

The questions surrounding the circumstances of his death and rushed burial have never been addressed. Pall was one more immigrant laborer, alone in this country. It's likely that many people assumed he had no family worth contacting. And in truth, it's unlikely any of his coworkers had the resources or the social standing to question the way in which his burial was quickly completed by local authorities. A rushed burial in a pauper's grave may have been a more common outcome for poor immigrants than we'd like to believe.

But what may have come of Pall's spirit? Some believe it remains at South Main School, working to complete that last job, the one that would book passage for his family to join him. Perhaps he's still there, mixing the mortar, lifting that last stone into place.

CONCLUSION

The next time you're driving around your own neighborhood, slow down a bit. Take notice of architecture that hearkens to our past. These structures offer a reflection of times gone by. They are monuments to history. Often, on closer inspection, they offer rich insights. If you are a believer in ghosts, you might see these old buildings as homes for wandering souls. Some souls, like that of Pall Forkos, are left with unfinished business as their most ardent desires have gone unfulfilled. Others, perhaps like Lester McCool, may yearn for simpler times, a desire to relive the happier moments of life.

Whatever the reason, let's hope that someday these souls find their way to whatever waits for them on the other side.

7
A TALE OF TONTOGANY

The greatest unsolved mysteries are the mysteries of our existence as conscious
beings in a small corner of a vast universe.
—*Freeman Dyson*

The village of Tontogany stands today on Wood County's northwestern edge. It's a community of just under four hundred residents. Living residents, that is. The tale that follows details the trials of those long dead, now buried in Tontogany Cemetery. At 1,500 registered burials, this cemetery's population is nearly four times the village's. The cemetery is situated off the banks of Tontogany Creek, in a flattened lot just north of town. Among its dead are early pioneers, Civil War veterans and countless ordinary citizens. Visitors can peruse the varied tombstones on the meticulously maintained grounds and wonder at the lives they represent.

Beyond that, many visitors wonder at something more, something difficult to explain. Many claim to witness strange hovering lights that linger over graves. Some have watched them blink and dance along the rows of tombstones. Even more common, however, are claims attached to the utility shed located on the grounds. Eerie blue lights are known to emanate from inside it. The shed's heavy, wide door has been seen opening and closing on its own on windless days. More recently, claims of full-sized shadow figures have been bandied about; their appearance leaves unsuspecting visitors with a terrible shock. Visits to loved ones' grave sites are sometimes interrupted by such encounters.

Wide-angle view of Tontogany Cemetery, September 2022.

One local woman recalled childhood memories of visiting the cemetery. One day, she tagged along with her parents to pay tribute to deceased family members. She couldn't shake the feeling of being watched by an unexplained presence hovering over her shoulder. In the same vein, several ghost hunters have investigated the site, walking away with photos of the unexplained lights leaving trails in their wake as they bounce and sway.

Claims of hauntings in old cemeteries are about as common as robins in spring. Many readers may be unimpressed with the trite setup, and for good reason. When it comes to legendary stories, this one might seem a bit unimaginative on the surface. But by digging a little deeper into the lives of a handful of souls buried beneath this Wood County soil, we discover a murderous history that once riveted locals, not to mention the nation.

It seems that restless spirits remain in this placid spot, and for good reason.

CURIOUS VISITS

The air was laden with a heavy dampness that late night on February 28, 1895. Dr. Adam Eddmon wrapped himself in his heaviest overcoat before

heading out into the dark. His wife, Catherine, and servant girl, Nellie Hartsing, had retired a couple hours earlier. Their rhythmic breathing proved the depth of their slumber. He had no doubt they'd sleep for hours more. Stepping out the front door, the good doctor's heels struck the wooden planks of an elegant front porch. His stately home stood on Washington Street, just a stone's throw from his office/drugstore on the corner of Broad and Main. Bracing himself against the moist night air, Dr. Eddmon slipped out into the night, turning east toward Tontogany Road. Without a soul in sight, he hurried on, anticipating his quick arrival at the home of Peter and Olive "Ollie" Peaney.

At fifty-two, Peter Peaney had spent his career as the town barber. After years of building a clientele with his shop next to the doctor's drugstore, he came to realize the savings on rent by simply barbering out of his own living room. And this he did, welcoming customers at his front stoop and ushering them in for a cut or a shave, whatever they desired. By that measure, not much was unusual about Dr. Edmon's unannounced visit—except that it was 11:00 p.m.

Just before reaching the Peaney home, Dr. Eddmon crossed the front yard of the Arnold residence next door. They'd been neighbors to the Peaneys for eight years. Both Mr. and Mrs. Arnold, and their young adult daughter Edna, had become accustomed to Dr. Eddmon's frequent if oddly timed

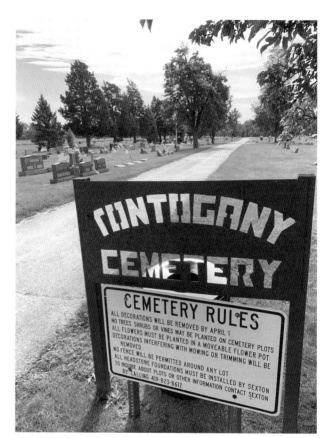

Right: Entrance to Tontogany Cemetery, September 2022.

Below: Utility shed at Tontogany Cemetery, September 2022.

Opposite: Artistic illustration of Dr. Adam Eddmon, as derived from a known photograph.

visits. That night, Edna had been up sick, unable to sleep. She'd caught sight of the Peaneys' downstairs light flickering on just after Dr. Eddmon rapped on their front door. It was yet another visit from the doctor who claimed to be one of Peter's most regular customers. Edna had often seen Dr. Eddmon arrive late at night, long after most sensible residents had gone to bed. Curiously, she'd also seen him arrive on days Peter was out of town. But the door always opened to him. Edna had her own theories as to the reasons for these visits.

Many residents whispered about the good doctor's *actual* relationship with the couple. Rumors had been circulating for some time.

Ollie Peaney was the only one who could have let him in when her husband wasn't home. Yet on this night, she did not allow him entry. Instead, Dr. Eddmon stood awkwardly at the stoop, shivering. He waited as Ollie climbed the stairs to her husband's bedroom. Waking him, she told him that Dr. Eddmon wanted a shave. Peter stumbled down the narrow wooden stairs, trying to shake off his sleep, and soon welcomed Eddmon through the front door. By then, Ollie had hurried to her first-floor bedroom, wanting no contact with the doctor who'd become as familiar to them as family.

A REVERED LEADER

Dr. Adam Eddmon's reputation prior to these described events had been impeccable. Many lionized him. Although he'd been a community leader in Tontogany for decades, including serving as mayor and a member of the school board, his history prior to planting roots in the town was nothing short of remarkable. Born to German immigrants in Philadelphia, he lost both parents by the time he was five. Taken in by relatives in Germany, he later followed in his deceased father's footsteps. He earned a medical degree at Halle University in Germany in 1868 before accepting a position as a staff surgeon on passenger ships that carried immigrants around the world. The job allowed him to see the globe, places like Chile and Tahiti. In San Francisco, he took an apprenticeship at a pharmacy, learning how to run a

Panoramic view of downtown Tontogany, intersection of Main and Broad Streets, September 2022.

drugstore. After recovering from a bout of smallpox, Eddmon decided to stay in America with hopes of opening his own pharmacy in Chicago. With some of the worst timing possible, he arrived in the city only a week before the Great Fire of 1871.

Further trials and tribulations brought him back to Germany and then again to the United States. He completed advanced training at the Physio-Eclectic Medical College in Cincinnati in 1877 before settling in Custar, Ohio. There for only a few months, he soon moved to Tontogany, where he would remain the rest of his life. He opened a drugstore/physician's office in this tiny village.

It would later become the scene of the murder of one of his most familiar patients.

In 1879, nearly two decades before that unspeakable day, Dr. Eddmon married Catherine Black, sister of the famed Captain Luther Black. Captain Black was a war hero who led troops against Confederate forces in Virginia. He was captured and suffered four months at a prisoner-of-war camp. After he finally reached home, Eddmon's future brother-in-law won a seat as the Wood County treasurer and was selected as a delegate to the Republican National Convention. He then struck it rich in the drug, oil and clothing industries. To put it briefly, Dr. and Mrs. Eddmon's marriage was a joining of families of prestige, wealth and local fame.

By 1887, Dr. Eddmon had been appointed special agent for the Cincinnati, Hamilton and Dayton Railroad (CH&D). All rail traffic through Tontogany had to be approved by him. He'd also been appointed to the boards of many charitable organizations and medical societies. There weren't many happenings in Wood County that Dr. Eddmon didn't influence. This fine reputation made what was to come all the more salacious.

A MURDER MOST FOUL

By March 1, 1895, a young woman by the name of Nellie Hartsing had been serving as Dr. and Mrs. Eddmon's live-in house servant for two years. On that night, she was dressing for bed when she heard what sounded like a gunshot out in the street. A woman's tortured moans soon followed. Startled, Nellie climbed the stairs to the master bedroom to wake Mrs. Eddmon, who had retired to bed hours earlier. The women whispered in the darkness, not knowing whether the shooter remained nearby. They debated whether one or the other of them should approach the front-facing windows of the home to investigate further. Before they could reach a decision, Dr. Eddmon flung wide the massive oak entry door and closed it quickly behind him. He had just hurried home from his nearby drugstore, clutching the knapsack that held the day's earnings. He was breathless. His face was turned up in a frenzy as sweat trailed down his cheeks; all this despite the brisk late-winter chill.

"Did you hear the gunshot?" were Eddmon's first words on finding Nellie and his wife huddling in the master bedroom.

Nellie acknowledged that she had and that she went to wake Mrs. Eddmon, who had somehow slept through it. In a rush, Eddmon explained that the shot sounded like it came from very near his office and that it happened as he was inside counting the day's receipts. Afraid of investigating the scene alone, he hurriedly locked up and scrambled the short distance home to check on the women's safety. The three of them then stared at one another, considering what steps to take next. They soon decided to venture onto the front porch. On doing so, their gazes turned in the direction of the drugstore a half block away. From around its back corner came a flickering glow. The sight was surreal at first, as though some self-illuminating object stood just around the corner, out of view. After they had stared for some moments, brief yet undeniable flames jutted into view.

"Fire!" Mrs. Eddmon was the first to yell it. "Fire!" she repeated, louder, in hopes of waking the neighbors who, like her, had slept through the gunshot. Within moments, Civil War veteran Captain Harry Rudd, the old man who lived across the street, ran out of his house and headed toward them. By the time he reached them, Eddmon had started filling two pails of water with the hand pump in his front yard. Flames two feet high were now plainly visible.

Rudd offered to go with the doctor to investigate. Oddly, Eddmon hesitated. The pails he held were now full and heavy in each hand. He stuttered when responding to the offer of help. Eddmon claimed fear of what they might encounter. Stooping down, Rudd grasped a brick from the ground near the water pump. He'd use it as a defensive weapon if needed. Mrs. Eddmon pleaded with the men to stay put. She, too, feared that an assailant might yet be lurking in the darkened streets. In the end, the two men approached the dancing flames together, mustering what fortitude they could.

On arriving at the fire, both saw what looked to be a pile of rubbish burning just outside the back door of the drugstore. They doused the flames, extinguishing the fire but also their only source of light on that moonless night. Luckily, by then, the commotion had roused more neighbors, and a small crowd began to gather at the scene. Soon enough, one man brought a lantern and held it to the burned remains still heaped on the ground. It was Frank Stevens, a man who lived a couple doors down from Rudd. Holding his face close in the lantern's glow, he leapt back in horror. The heap was no pile of rubbish.

It was Ollie Peaney.

The bodice of her dress smoldered from the collar down to the waist. It was the same dress she was wearing when she stopped by Stevens's house earlier that day. Ollie and her husband, Peter, were known to play cards with the Stevenses, and Ollie had stopped in to invite them over that night. Stevens stammered, repeating that he had seen the dead woman earlier that same day. In a state of shock, the three men lifted her corpse out of the puddle of water to move her a few feet onto dry ground.

"I heard a gunshot as I was counting up receipts," Eddmon mumbled as Stevens once again inspected the poor woman's charred remains. It was time to call the authorities.

Both Rudd and Eddmon rushed to Marshal William Crum's home to wake him. By the time the three of them returned to the scene, a growing crowd had to be pushed back. On appointing a few trustworthy onlookers to keep the scene secured, the marshal headed for the Peaney house, where it was presumed Peter would be found. But when the marshal rapped loudly on the barber's front door, no one answered. Crum ran back to the scene of the crime, announcing that Ollie's husband was not at home. As a primary person of interest, it was assumed he was at large.

An anxious murmur rippled through the crowd. Folks offered theories on the motives, means and circumstances of the crime. It was then that Dr. Collins, a fellow Tontogany physician, leaned toward Eddmon and whispered his suggestion that the two of them head to the Peaney house together. Eddmon once again hesitated, just as he had done with Rudd. In the end, he agreed.

The doctors arrived in no time at the Peaney household, which was two-tenths of a mile away. As with Marshal Crum, their rapping on the front door went unanswered. But with a turn of the knob from the outside, the door popped open. For a nervous moment the men held each other's gaze. Collins was the first to step over the threshold and into the Peaneys' kitchen. Eddmon protested, to no avail. Collins stepped into the downstairs bedroom and found the bed's covers turned up. The pillow looked as if someone had placed a hand in the middle of it. Eddmon reluctantly followed Collins into the home. He explained that this was Ollie's bedroom, that she slept separately from her husband on account of his snoring. Taken a bit aback, Collins asked just how Eddmon knew all this. Without answering, Eddmon stepped back into the kitchen. He pointed out Peter's damp clothes drying by the stove, a sure sign that Peter was home, probably sleeping in his own bedroom upstairs. Collins then opened the wooden door that led to a narrow stairway. He called loudly for the barber. No response. He took the lantern Eddmon had been carrying and climbed the stairs alone. There, beneath heavy quilts, was a sleeping Peter Peaney. It took Collins considerable effort to rouse him. After the initial confusion wore off and he recognized Dr. Collins, Peaney explained that the last thing he remembered was going to bed at 8:30 p.m.

On hearing both men's voices, Eddmon climbed up the stairs. He stepped nervously into the room and placed a hand on the barber's shoulder. He cut to the chase: "Pete, a woman is dead downtown, and some think it is Ollie. I don't know whether it is or not."

Eddmon *did* know. He just couldn't bear to say so. Collins didn't correct him.

Peter then got dressed, and the three men headed to the scene.

THE PEANEYS

Peter and Ollie Peaney had lived together for twenty years in a common-law marriage. Peter, the fifty-two-year-old barber, hailed from Blissfield, Michigan. More than two decades prior to the murder, he had somehow crossed paths with then twenty-four-year-old Ollie Bernthisel. This young woman was native to another Wood County hamlet, Haskins. She would come to live with Peaney in Tontogany. The couple was well known among the locals, as most everyone knew everyone in such a small community. They'd grown particularly close with Dr. Eddmon and his wife. Besides being a regular customer, the doctor served as a business advisor to Peter.

Mrs. Eddmon considered herself a close personal friend of Ollie's. Despite these wholesome connections, rumors abounded as to the true purpose of Ollie and Dr. Eddmon's frequent visits with each other. Dr. Eddmon, for his part, was known to stop by the Peaney home at all times of day and night, long after any reasonable barber would accept walk-ins. His last visit occurred on the evening before her death. For some reason, Eddmon had not been welcomed in on that night, unlike so many other nights. That night, Ollie left the good doctor to stand in the cold. She'd let her husband do the entertaining, having no apparent interest in it.

What wasn't quite as well known to the locals, however, were Ollie's frequent trips to the drugstore long after night had fallen, even as late as 1:00 a.m. And on the afternoon of her murder, multiple residents had seen her walking the streets. One local by the name of George Mathews recalled spotting her around 3:30 p.m. that day walking down Washington Street toward the drugstore. He caught up with her to chat in an effort to be neighborly and was surprised at her aloof response. She acted "queer, like an insane person," he was later quoted in the press.

Peter Peaney, for his part, would also recall his wife's peculiar behavior on the night before and the day of her murder. He thought it odd that she at first refused Dr. Eddmon's entry to their home. She customarily let Eddmon in to get settled before coming up to wake him. He was the only customer Peter would shave so late. Peter felt an odd tension from Ollie that night. Her strange demeanor continued the following day, when she sat in silence as they ate supper. She was distant and closed off from him. He remembered hoping her mood would improve once the Stevenses arrived to play cards. When hours passed and no company arrived, Peter decided to head to bed at 8:30. He had assumed his wife had done the same. The next thing he knew, a pair of doctors had come to wake him and brought him to his dead wife.

An Investigation Commences

Before the doctors and Peaney could make it to the scene, Marshal Crum had telephoned the coroner's office in Toledo. Coroner Thomas received the lawman's call. By 1:00 a.m., he had headed out of the city in a handcar. By the time he made it to Tontogany, Deputy Sheriff Alf Farmer was also present to assist Marshal Crum with the initial investigative efforts.

Ollie's charred body lay diagonally just a few feet from the back entrance to Dr. Eddmon's drugstore. She'd initially fallen on the stoop, her body later dragged out of the puddle of water used to extinguish the flames. Coroner Thomas requested assistance in finding a space to perform an autopsy. Drs. Collins and Eddmon agreed to assist with the procedure. Her body was transported to the local undertaker's office. It was there, under gaslit lamps, that the true cause of her death was discovered. A .32-caliber bullet had entered the throat just above the sternum and passed through the left auricle of the heart. It lodged below the shoulder blade, from where it was later extracted. The bullet's trajectory indicated that the gun was held at an angle above her at extremely close range. Thomas theorized that she may have stooped down in a feeble attempt to avoid the shot. More evidence indicated she'd made attempts at a defense. Her right wrist and the back of her right hand were badly burned by gunpowder, indicating that she probably threw up her hand as the shot was fired. The fire started as flames about her throat, likely ignited by the expended gunpowder at such close range. Death was caused by the severing of the carotid artery two inches from the heart. She would have lost consciousness instantaneously, dying within three to four minutes.

Suicide was categorically ruled out. All signs pointed to homicide. Coroner Thomas stayed the weekend, through March 4, conducting exhaustive interviews of all witnesses.

On questioning, Dr. Eddmon restated what he had told his wife and Nellie Hartsing: that he had been alone in the drugstore counting up the day's receipts and just getting ready to lock up when he heard a nearby gunshot at about 9:48 p.m. He claimed to have no knowledge that anyone had died, let alone Ollie Peaney, until extinguishing what he and Captain Rudd believed to be a pile of burning rubbish. He acknowledged knowing the Peaneys well. In fact, he had been treating Ollie for heart problems. She was known to seek emergency treatment when a bout of panic and shortness of breath began. This testimony was confirmed by her husband and others who were aware of Ollie's health problems. Many had observed her suffer heart troubles in person. What was unexplainable, however, was that Ollie was not known to seek Dr. Eddmon's emergency care without first telling her husband.

The initial investigation did not definitively identify any suspects but left most assuming that Ollie's husband was the most likely culprit. He was summarily arrested by Sheriff Richard Biggs and brought to the Wood County jail by train. By then, the investigation had been handed over from the coroner to the sheriff. With this development, Ollie's father, Henry Bernthisel of Haskins, hired a special detective at his own expense to work in concert with the sheriff's department.

Under questioning, Peter Peaney adamantly denied having any part in his wife's murder. He also denied having any guns. But a search of his property and properties nearby turned up what was, at that time, believed to be the murder weapon. In the Arnold house, next door to the Peaneys, in an upstairs bureau was found a .32-caliber double-action Harrington & Richardson revolver. When a deputy brought it downstairs to Mrs. Arnold, she broke into tears and confessed that a woman by the name of Mrs. Garrett (Ollie's half sister) had brought the weapon to her from the Peaney house only days earlier. It had been stored on the Peaneys' mantel. Against Mrs. Arnold's wishes, Mrs. Garrett stashed it upstairs in the bureau drawer, where the deputy later found it. All chambers were loaded. Mrs. Garrett had been staying with her brother-in-law in the days since Ollie's murder. Immediately after storing the gun at the neighbor's house, she boarded a train back to her home in Toledo.

This evidence became even more damning considering multiple accounts offered by neighbors about the Peaneys' strained marriage. It was claimed that Peter had a jealous disposition and that he frequently argued with his wife. One neighbor, Wesley Arnold, claimed that a very loud argument could be heard from inside the Peaney home the night before Ollie's murder. Peter, for his part, adamantly denied any marital problems. He knew his wife's heart problems well and was thankful for Dr. Eddmon's efforts in treating her. He did think it odd, however, that she didn't wake him to say she was headed to his office the night she died.

With all these tantalizing claims, gossip ran hot as to who killed Ollie and why. Many believed that Peter Peaney did it. These suspicions cooled when forensic evidence surfaced. Ballistics tests revealed that the Peaneys' revolver found in the Arnolds' upstairs bureau had never, in fact, been fired. The visiting Mrs. Garrett had taken it upon herself to remove the unused gun. She had feared its mere presence would bring unwanted suspicion. With no other leads, Sheriff Biggs took what many assumed to be the only course of action left.

The House Servant, Charged

With the evidence against Peter Peaney drying up, a new motive began forming in the minds of lawmen and ordinary townspeople alike. Juicy tales of Dr. Eddmon's lustful relationship with his young house servant took center stage. It was alleged that the doctor's young paramour had grown envious of Ollie Peaney's frequent visits to the drugstore late at night. Detectives on the case heard claims from multiple residents about what they believed to be a sordid love triangle gone awry. On nothing but hearsay, Nellie Hartsing was arrested and set for arraignment. Court documents detail Hartsing as a comely looking lady with a frank countenance. Her womanly grace was quiet and unassuming. Prosecutor Murphy read a statement aloud to the court, accusing her of firing the shot that ended Ollie Peaney's life. Hartsing burst into tears in the courtroom, denying any intimacies with Dr. Eddmon and claiming that she viewed him and Mrs. Eddmon as her employers only. She pleaded not guilty. Within a matter of days, the prosecutor was forced to admit he lacked enough evidence to detain her, much less prosecute her. Hartsing was released from all charges. There was much speculation that her arrest was being used as a cover for more sensational developments to come.

Back to the Drawing Board

In desperation, as all feared that Ollie Peaney's murderer might never be identified, Wood County commissioners offered a $500 reward for anyone with information leading to the conviction of the guilty party. Dr. Eddmon, for his part, hired a hotshot detective out of Saginaw, Michigan, to aid with the case. Rumors multiplied, however, that the good doctor was only taking these efforts to throw suspicion away from himself.

Three months after Ollie Peaney fell dead at the back door of Dr. Eddmon's drugstore, a grand jury returned indictments for murder on both the doctor and his wife. The grand jury had reviewed over two hundred witness statements and eleven true bills. Arrest warrants were issued. Sheriff Biggs and Deputies Farmer and Hemphill traveled to Tontogany to carry out the warrants. When the lawmen brought the couple out of their stately home in handcuffs, a crowd gathered and gawked. Mrs. Eddmon remained calm, but Dr. Eddmon's emotions spilled over. Nellie Hartsing cried as her employers were put into waiting cars. On finally reaching Bowling Green, they were placed in separate cells on separate floors. There would be no bail set for murder charges.

Dr. and Mrs. Eddmon were arraigned the next day, both pleading not guilty. The case garnered intense media attention across Northwest Ohio and the country at large. Locals came to the courthouse hours early to grab a good seat for the proceedings. Latecomers accepted standing-room-only positions to watch the developments. Some believed the doctor and his wife were innocent. Many now questioned the real motives of the man they thought they knew, the man who had treated their ills and healed their wounds for so many years.

Trial dates were set for Dr. Eddmon on July 8 and Mrs. Eddmon on July 28. Dr. Eddmon's drugstore was placed under the charge of Jerry City pharmacist Dr. D.C. Whitehead.

On Trial for His Life

The crowded courtroom was stifling on July 10, 1895. A calm and composed Dr. Eddmon sat at the defendant's table with his famous and wealthy brother-in-law. Captain Black hired the high-priced attorneys who sat next to them.

Prosecutor Murphy opened with a statement, proclaiming the Peaney household a peaceful one. Husband Peter Peaney was found to be the congenial town barber who offered services out of his home. He'd slept upstairs to save his wife from his dreadful snoring. Dr. Eddmon was well known to the couple, as they often exchanged visits at late hours. Ollie Peaney enjoyed the doctor's company and had even offered to serve as nurse for some of his more challenging patients. On the afternoon of her last day alive, March 1, 1895, multiple witnesses saw Ollie in Dr. Eddmon's drugstore. Another observer saw her walking down the street around 9:30 p.m., about twenty minutes before the gunshot rang out. Murphy vowed to present a case demonstrating Eddmon's guilt. There was no doubt he'd pulled the trigger.

The defense, for its part, dismissed the notion of Eddmon's guilt out of hand. All the state's evidence was circumstantial. Authorities tried arresting Peter Peaney first, then the Eddmon's house servant, Nellie Hartsing. Both were eventually released due to a lack of evidence. This proved the prosecutor's pattern of incompetence and sheer conjecture as to who killed this poor woman. And to top that off, Mrs. Eddmon remained in jail awaiting her own trial. She'd been kept in a separate cell, having not seen her husband for weeks. Just who did the state think pulled the trigger, Dr. Eddmon or his wife? Clearly, the state did not know and simply hoped that if one prosecution didn't work, maybe the other would.

With the opening arguments finished, the day's proceedings closed. Testimonies of more than one hundred witnesses began the next morning. Among the most notable testimonies included that of Mrs. Clara Arnold, of the family that lived next door to the Peaneys for eight years. She testified that Dr. Eddmon was known to visit the Peaney home late at night after Peter Peaney had gone to bed. She'd also seen him arrive when the barber was out of town. She knew of Ollie's history of heart problems but demurred when the prosecutor asked why she thought the doctor had made so many late-night visits.

Alfred Plotner, who lived only a few doors down from the drugstore, recalled seeing Ollie earlier that day walking down the street. She was being followed by an unknown man who kept pace nearly ten feet behind her. Plotner thought the situation odd, as he knew everyone in town. The defense dug deeper into this mysterious development, calling additional witnesses who also claimed to have observed the suspicious stranger. In a bit of courtroom drama, it was revealed that Ollie had in fact been previously married. At the age of nineteen, long before she'd met Peter Peaney, Ollie had made her way to St. Louis and married a German immigrant by the name of Robert Beurns. It was further revealed that she'd borne him a child, whom she abandoned when she returned to live in Ohio. No divorce records could be found, indicating that Ollie remained legally married to Mr. Beurns. She had lived with her common-law husband, Peter Peaney, for the past twenty years.

Multiple witnesses detailed the peculiar arrival of a stranger to town two months before Ollie's murder. He called himself "Dennis," spoke with a German accent and planned to set up a blacksmith shop in town. Some local tradesmen helped him get started, loaning him the necessary equipment. This man was oddly quiet and withdrawn, offering no details of his background or just why he chose Tontogany to set up shop. Curiously, "Dennis" had not joined the crowd that night at the scene of the murder. More curious was the fact that he'd simply disappeared on that night. Inside his shop were found half-completed projects. He had left just as mysteriously as he had come.

Could a spurned, jealous husband, after twenty years, muster a rage that could result in cold-blooded murder on the streets of Tontogany? The defense argued it was entirely plausible.

While these tantalizing developments caused a stir, the prosecution began tackling Dr. Eddmon's credibility. One after another, witnesses told conflicting stories about what Eddmon had said to them regarding his exact whereabouts when the gun was fired. He told some that he was counting up the day's receipts inside the store. He told others that he had already locked up and was walking home when the shot rang out. He told yet another man that he was on a fifteen-minute stroll uptown to get some fresh air and, when the shot rang out, headed for his store. These inconsistencies became a centerpiece of the state's argument for conviction.

On the heels of this argument came forensic evidence from the scene itself. The alley leading to the store's back entrance was wet and muddy that night. In order for Ollie to have approached the back door, she would have had to walk down the alley, leaving footprints. None were found by detectives on the scene. This meant that she had to have been let in through the front door and later shot at the back stoop.

Dr. Eddmon would have been alone in his store that night, having closed hours before.

Adding to its momentum, the prosecution brought one witness after another who reported it was common knowledge that Dr. Eddmon kept at least two revolvers at his store, one stashed at each entrance. Peter Peaney was one of the witnesses who described the revolvers as big with black handles. One of Dr. Eddmon's former house servants claimed the doctor slept with a revolver under his pillow. She'd seen him carry it with him to the drugstore. Eddmon had in fact turned over two .38-caliber revolvers to the sheriff early in the investigation. But these firearms did not match the witnesses' descriptions of what they knew to be his guns. The weapon that killed Ollie Peaney was a larger .32-caliber revolver.

In especially stinging testimony, Marshal Crum claimed he knew for certain that Dr. Eddmon owned .32-caliber revolvers. He'd seen him carry them. He also recalled a special detail from the immediate investigation that night. The marshal had smelled spent gunpowder in the oil room, which stood at the back of the drugstore and led to the back door.

Sheriff's deputies testified to a field test they had completed at the Wood County Fairgrounds. In reenacting the scene, they shoot a .32 revolver into a dress-wearing manikin. They shot at point-blank range, downward at about eight inches from the throat. The spark did indeed ignite the fabric, which soon turned into a blaze. In dramatic fashion, after explaining the test, the jury was presented with the actual dress Ollie had been wearing. Most of what remained was the full skirt. Its bodice lay in charred pieces, barely recognizable. And to make a fine point, Prosecutor Murphy presented the bullet that had been extracted from her lifeless body. He was certain it came from Dr. Eddmon's gun, its whereabouts yet unknown. Surely the doctor had been the one to pull the trigger.

DEFENSE'S ARGUMENTS

Dr. Eddmon's high-powered attorneys attacked the state's arguments from multiple angles, working to create any smidgin of doubt that could lead to an acquittal. First, the state failed to explain any motive Dr. Eddmon might have had. Even if there were an illicit love affair between he and Ollie, as the prosecution intimated many times, Eddmon would have been protective of his lover, not murderous toward her. And in what seemed a kind of concession, the defense acknowledged the likelihood of a forbidden affair when they took to calling Peter Peaney a "knave, villain cuckhold." In yet another approach, they drew attention to Ollie's estranged first husband and the mysterious German-speaking "Dennis" who skipped town right after the murder.

The Eddmons and the Peaneys had been friends for years. And men don't kill their friends, the defense argued. Attorney Baldwin's closing statement was recorded as such, "I tell you when you take such men as Dr. Eddmon and hang them up to a gibbet, you are taking from the community the best man that can aid in making this glorious country what it is today."

The defense rested.

PROSECUTION'S ARGUMENTS

The prosecution repeated its assertions, considered irrefutable, that it claimed led to one conclusion. Ollie Peaney had to have come into the drugstore through the front door. Dr. Eddmon acknowledged he'd been alone there that night. He'd had the means to kill her and in fact was the only person there who could have done it. For all the squawking the defense made about circumstantial evidence, they'd not put forward any alternative for who could have been there, inside the store.

Dr. Eddmon couldn't keep his story straight as to exactly what he was doing when the gunshot rang out. His claims evolved over time. He told some people that he'd been counting the money, told others that he was already headed home and told yet others he was on a walk around town.

Ollie's behavior was viewed as strange by her husband and by friends and acquaintances who saw her earlier that day. She'd refused to let Dr. Eddmon in on his last late-night visit to the Peaney home. Something was off well before she fell from the bullet that would take her life.

In conclusion, Attorney Troup made his closing argument: "You have been told that you cannot convict because of a lack of a motive. But there was a motive. I do not propose to call harsh names, but I want to call attention to the weakness of human nature. You don't need to be told that there were improper relations between Dr. Eddmon and Mrs. Peaney. You know that beyond a doubt. And I want to tell you that when two married people enter into such relations, there will follow, sooner or later, serious trouble and oft times murder."

In Conclusion

NOT GUILTY.

Dr. Eddmon Acquitted of the Murder of Mrs. Olive Peaney—Indictment Against Mrs. Eddmon Quashed.

TOLEDO, O., July 17.—Tuesday evening a jury of his peers, after a consultation of scarcely three-quarters of an hour returned a verdict declaring Dr. Adam Eddmon not guilty of the murder of Mrs. Olive Peaney. Following immediately on this came the announcement that the indictment against Mrs. Eddmon, who had been charged with the murder had been dismissed at the instance of Prosecuting Attorney Murphy, of Wood county. Thus the now famous case is as much a mystery as it was two months ago and the probabilities are that the murderers will never be discovered.

On the night of March 21 last Mrs. Olive Peany, the wife of the village barber of Tontogany, a hamlet of six hundred population, was found murdered at the rear of the drug store kept by Dr. Adam Eddmon. Death had been caused by a bullet wound in the heart and when the body was discovered the clothing of the murdered woman was ablaze.

Article from the *Chillicothe Gazette*, July 17, 1895. Newspapers.com.

Throughout the trial, some jurors outwardly displayed their emotions, silent tears streaming down their faces. Many claimed sickness on multiple occasions and asked that arguments be closed. The pressure they faced was considerable. Perhaps that's why it took just thirty minutes of deliberation. Wood County's iconic bell tower atop the courthouse rang out the clear signal that a verdict had been reached.

Not guilty.

In an unusual scene, once the audience was quieted and the trial declared adjourned, Dr. Eddmon stepped toward the jury box and shook the hands of all twelve jurors. His famous brother-in-law, Captain Black, followed behind him, offering hearty thanks for the acquittal.

So ended one of the most memorable trials in the annals of Wood County.

What Remains

The murder of Olive Peaney has now gone unsolved for more than 125 years. For decades, many believed Dr. Eddmon the guilty party. While the circumstantial evidence against him was considerable, it wasn't enough to convict him. Or was it? Some speculated that this wealthy and well-

Grave site of Ollie and Peter Peaney in Tontogany Cemetery, September 2022.

connected professional was simply able to pay his way out of the crime he committed. Some questioned the jury's lightning-fast deliberation. They questioned the doctor's chummy way of openly thanking each juror for their vote to acquit. Was there some undue influence? Had he somehow bribed them? How many of their family members had he treated and healed? And what's to be made of his roles as mayor and school board member? It's worth noting that during his trial, Dr. Eddmon was nominated to run for mayor of Tontogany once again. It's clear that Wood County residents loved him.

And what of Ollie Peaney? This poor woman lost the most. In death, she lost even what remained of her reputation. Perhaps some, including jurors, viewed her life as one marred by scandal. At a time when women couldn't vote or even sit on juries, the mere appearance of impropriety suggested that she deserved whatever fate befell her. If Ollie Peaney's ghost lingers near her final resting place, she may long for more than justice. She may long to set the record straight, to tell the story of a woman battling health problems and doing her best to cope with what life gave her.

She fled from her first husband. With her second, she made do.

Grave site of Adam and Catherine Eddmon in Tontogany Cemetery, September 2022.

Perhaps she found love in the arms of another, in the arms of Dr. Adam Eddmon. True or not, no one deserves to die in such a way.

Whatever the truth of the matter is, two people knew it: Ollie Peaney and her murderer. The spirits of these two are said to manifest as hovering, swaying lights in Tontogany Cemetery yet today. May they someday find rest, and may we learn from their past trials, not forgotten.

8

THE LEGEND
OF WOODBURY HOUSE

Monsters are real, and ghosts are real too.
They live inside us, and sometimes, they win.
—Stephen King

The tale of the Woodbury House is a unique topic for this book. It's a legend that's outlived the very structure itself. This notorious house was dismantled more than a century ago. Even the town in which it stood, Woodbury, has vanished without a trace. It's now the nondescript intersection of South Dixie Highway and Jerry City Road. A stone's throw from noisy I-75, the general vicinity contains about a dozen relatively modern residences. A contracting business located on the corner advertises services for those wishing to build new homes.

Nothing that remains here suggests that this spot once brought terror to even the hardest-edged settlers of the early nineteenth century.

While no evidence of the place is still visible, historical facts pertaining to the tale's protagonist have been revealed. Whether or not we're to believe that this long-demolished house was once haunted, we know the truth of those who once lived there. What's most surprising about this piece of folklore is that many details are verifiable. That's a trait not often found among centuries-old sensational stories.

The year was about 1820. Construction of what would become the Woodbury House had just been completed. The process had been a real labor, as was every task in that age. The foundation of the structure had to

Top: Satellite view of the intersection of South Dixie Highway and Jerry City Road. *Google Maps, imagery ©2022, Maxar Technologies, State of Ohio, OSIP, USDA/FPAC/GEO.*

Bottom: Artist's depiction of the Woodbury House.

be dug from the heavy sludge that was the Great Black Swamp. Not many immigrant settlers had the courage—or perhaps stupidity—to take on such a project in this godforsaken place. No neighbor could be spotted for miles. Mosquitos swarmed around men plunging shovels into the muddy mess, their feet sinking deeper with every thrust. It's a wonder anything ever got built here. It would have taken considerable determination to see the thing to completion.

Unfortunately, the original owner's name has been lost to time. No doubt, he was a man of means. It would have taken a lot of money to fund the construction of a home that locals would later call a mansion. The house's specifics, including the floor plan and architectural design, are also not known. We're left guessing at what a sight it must have been, especially in the early years. Imagine what transpired in the mind of an early traveler, trudging through endless miles of muck and insects, only to come upon a stately home inside a tiny clearing of trees.

Even before the place had ghosts, it was the talk of the town, as they say.

Although the original owner is unknown, at least one record exists as to those who later owned the property. The list includes celebrities of the time, including Dr. Alexander Duncan, a Democratic congressman from Cincinnati. He leased it out as an investment property, of all things. This home's reputation as a shining jewel within a dismal swamp was well known across the state.

DEEDS OF BLACKNESS WITHIN THE BLACK SWAMP

By the early 1850s, this unusual home had begun to take on a darker character. The then unoccupied structure was known for strange happenings, including ghostly moans and misty, vaporous shapes floating from room to room. Rumors that it was haunted spread far and wide, so much so that it became a kind of tourist attraction. In much the same spirit that ghost hunting is celebrated today, those with a spiritual curiosity sought this place out. One well-publicized account of an "investigation" of sorts was written by a man named Major Ward. He's assumed to have been a veteran of the War of 1812. It's his story, printed and reprinted in newspapers for decades, that serves as the basis of this telling.

While much of what Major Ward reports is far-fetched to say the least, other specifics he mentions are verifiable within the historical record. It seems he believed himself to be reporting the truth of his experience, whether or not he actually was. Whatever the case, it's a story that has lived on through the ages.

Let's see what all the fascination is about.

On May 15, 1853, Ward struck up an easy connection with a man named John Stow. The two had made each other's acquaintance at a local place called McCrory's Tavern. Just a few miles outside Woodbury, it was once an old rookery that had been repurposed as a drinking establishment. Over successive pints, the men rattled on about that supposedly haunted place down the road known as Woodbury House. Neither had ever been there, yet both had heard the stories passed around many times over. They'd heard tell of one former owner, John Cleves, who once rented a room to a passing peddler named Syms. This poor, elderly wandering salesman would meet his end there at the hands of the murderous owner. Rumors further held that John Cleves had years earlier served time in the Ohio Penitentiary for the crime of having had an incestuous relationship with his sister.

The gossip around this story was both scandalous and incessant.

The supposed crimes of murder and incest were accepted as truth by most. Once something is repeated often enough, it takes on a life all its own. As to the otherworldly claims, both Ward and Stow declared that they did not believe in hobgoblins. Neither had any fear of the home that so many never dared set foot in. As the conversation grew louder between them, the proprietor, McCrory himself, sauntered over to their table. He curtly advised the pair that if they wanted to see the place for themselves, he'd gladly take them. He knew it well and implied that he had unique knowledge of it. He just wasn't inclined to share it. He found it better to let newcomers experience Woodbury House with a fresh and open mind.

McCrory had thrown the gauntlet, in essence, and now each man was obliged to take it. Both agreed, happily, to the invitation. Over cheap cigars, the trio discussed the details of what would come next. They'd have to wait a couple of hours at least for the sun to finish setting and night to settle in.

In the meantime, Major Ward headed to his hotel room to grab his firearms. One was a horse pistol, the other a Colt six-shooter. He was convinced that whatever strange happenings occurred in the place came from a living source. Perhaps a local prankster was known to hide out in a darkened room for the pleasure of scaring the bejesus out of curious tourists. Or worse, it could all be a setup for a robbery. Whatever the case, the major would be prepared.

When 10:00 p.m. arrived, Ward and Stow met up at the tavern. McCrory's decrepit wagon was hitched and ready for the journey. They traveled the empty road in silence. On arriving, McCrory pulled back on the reins in front of the dilapidated, dark and empty house. In the glow of the moon, its decayed state didn't completely overwhelm the grandeur it once held. The three of them sat motionless for a bit, just soaking it all in, before the two adventure seekers unloaded themselves. Without a word, McCrory shook the major's hand in a gesture of goodbye before slapping the reins. The wheels creaked once more down the lonely dirt road as the wagon disappeared into the night.

The Investigation Begins

From the looks of it, the place had sat vacant for many years. The air was chilly and damp as the two men climbed the front steps toward the front entrance. Just before they entered, the thought occurred to Major Ward that they should have planned better. He was friends with an editor of the *Plain Dealer*. With a clearer mind he might have arranged for his friend to join as a third witness (one with access to a printing press to boot). As the situation stood, the pair would have to confront whatever came at them. With only a lantern to guide them through the drafty, dusty rooms, they'd eventually sit on the floor in the main living space. What little furniture remained in the home was too rotted for use. They started a fire with a few boards they found lying near the fireplace and extinguished the lantern. To stave off sleep, they lit cigars.

They puffed and waited and puffed and waited.

As the proverbial hour of midnight approached, the undeniable figure of a human skeleton drifted into the room, startling the men to their feet. The major yelled, demanding to know the figure's identity and purpose. It gave no response other than to continue gliding toward the center of the room, where it stopped. Stow, for his part, retreated to a back corner. The two had decided to take these positions per an earlier conversation should anything

Artist's depiction of Major Ward and John Stow's ghostly encounter at Woodbury House.

present itself. This way, Stow would have a full view of what was happening and a vantage point for their defense.

Despite the remarkable sight, the major remained convinced that someone was putting them on. It had to be a trick of light and shadows causing the apparition to appear. When the figure remained unresponsive to his commands, he raised a pistol to its chest and fired. The bullet sank deep into the opposite wall as the figure began advancing toward him. A second bullet met the same end, and the figure came to within an arm's length. By then, Major Ward was stunned into silence as he scrutinized the hovering, transparent skeleton before him. After a moment, he waved for Stow to come closer, and the two men traded places as the thing remained silent and motionless.

All at once, the figure moved to the fireplace and then back to the center of the room. Raising a hand, it began to speak aloud. It said his name was James Syms, born in Augusta, Georgia. He'd fought for General Anthony Wayne, battling Indian forces on the outskirts of the forest. Lastly, he said was sixty-eight years old when he died.

The major asked whether he'd been murdered there in Woodbury House. The figure, or perhaps we should call it Syms, admonished him to ask no questions. It continued explaining that on an evening in December 1841, he'd rented a room from one John Cleves. At some point after falling asleep in bed, he was struck with a blow to the side of his head. Before losing full consciousness, he'd gotten a glimpse of Cleves's face as he held some blunt object above him. In Syms's struggle to get to his feet, he was met with another blow to the temple, which killed him. In so explaining, the ghostly Syms turned the side of his skull to the men, revealing a long and jagged fracture where the blow had landed.

The second blow had killed him, sending his spirit rising above his lifeless body. He recalled watching Cleves from above as he continued pounding on his lifeless corpse. After many blows, Cleves finally stopped and began the work of severing the head from the body with the axe he'd used to kill him. When the dismembering was done, Cleves lifted some floorboards and buried the head beneath where Ward and Stow now stood. Cleves then hauled the body out to a nearby well, which he filled in that same night, concealing the place of the burial.

THE HEAD LIES BENEATH

Syms had haunted the place ever since his gruesome death. All these years, he'd waited for just the right living soul or two to come along to ask them to free his head from beneath the floor. He told them to start by removing a couple bricks from the hearth and then pry some adjacent boards loose, exposing his cranium.

The men set to work as instructed and found the skull quickly. In amazement, Major Ward held the thing in his hands as he turned it over, exposing the long, jagged fracture on one side, just where he expected it to be. And in another hard-to-fathom claim from his account, Ward says that the skull somehow disappeared from his hands and then reappeared atop Syms's shoulders, becoming fused within the ghostly figure so that what was once solid bone was now one with the transparent mist.

Syms then spoke to them once more. He explained that after the evil deed was done, Cleves used his keys to unlock the trunks he used to store his wares. He rifled through the items as though taking an inventory. He stole ninety dollars he'd been carrying, his total life savings. And then he loaded up all the possessions into the peddler's wagon. Driving through the night, he'd arrive at a nearby Indian village by dawn. He sold the entire lot, including Syms's horse and wagon, to the tribal leader. Cleves then headed home with what seemed to be a guilt-free conscience.

Not long after the murder, John Cleves was tried and convicted of a separate crime, of having an incestuous relationship with his sister. He was sent to the Ohio Penitentiary and later released, but he'd gotten away with the slaying. No one from Wood County knew of the traveling salesman, so there was no one to miss him when he was gone. Syms's death—and seemingly his life—had been forgotten by all except the lonely spirit left haunting Woodbury House.

Syms believed he wouldn't be able to fully cross the veil until his death was recognized and his murderer punished. He implored the men to find his family still living in Georgia to tell them he'd been killed. Once notified, he was sure they wouldn't stop until Cleves was tried and hanged for the crime. He also asked for a proper burial in a dedicated grave, with a stone to mark that he once lived and was not forgotten.

Another Mystery Revealed

After hearing Syms's plea, Ward took a moment before making an ultimatum. He'd only complete the task if Syms would first answer one question. It was a question only a spirit might be able to answer. For decades, many had tried to solve the mystery of the strange disappearance of Theodosia Burr Alston, the daughter of the one and only Aaron Burr. She'd grown up to marry the governor of South Carolina, expanding her credentials as a celebrity. When she inexplicably disappeared during a sea voyage to New York in 1813, rumors abounded as to just what happened to the vibrant twenty-nine-year-old woman. Some believed her ship had run into pirates known to prowl the Eastern Seaboard. Others thought her ship had most likely wrecked somewhere in the vast expanse. By the middle of the nineteenth century, the enigma had taken on a life of its own, not unlike our view of Amelia Earhart's fate today. Had Theodosia been forced to walk the plank in a stormy sea? Or had she been taken hostage and later accepted among the ranks of pirates? Did her ghost haunt the rocky shoreline of the Carolinas, calling forth ships to their own doom on the rocks?

It was this opportunity that Major Ward took to ask the ghostly Syms what came of Theodosia Burr. Syms didn't hesitate, quickly confirming that she had met a gruesome death not unlike his own. After her ship was boarded by pirates, her death came swift and sudden, with the blow of something heavy to her head. Syms confirmed that her spirit now rested, as he so wished to do. And with this, Syms held out his bony hand to confirm their deal. Major Ward reached out to shake it. As his fingers wrapped around the ghostly hand, passing through it, a cold chill surged up his arm. With a clap of distant thunder and a strange flash of a blue light, Syms vanished before them.

A Fantastic Story and Nothing More, Right?

Great ghost tales such as this are as old as time. Elements of this story in particular echo the premise of Shakespeare's *Hamlet*, involving a man tasked to right his father's death by the ghost of the father himself. It's a plot that resonates with the audience on both spiritual and emotional levels. Beyond that, the legend of Woodbury House has a tantalizing setup. This archetypal haunted house had drawn visitors from all corners. People were curious about the mansion already. More than just a creepy story, this tale has a talking specter who, by the way, shares the secret of the biggest unsolved mystery of that time.

It's no wonder this story was printed and reprinted in newspapers all over the region. Great fiction tends to have a long shelf life, right?

SEPARATING FACT FROM FICTION

James Syms, the doomed spirit we met as a wispy, talking skeleton in Major Ward's story, claims to have fought against Indian forces during the War of 1812. This military service supposedly came long before his untimely death in 1841. Remarkably, a man by the same name is listed on the historical rolls of Colonel William Dudley's mounted battalion. These rolls are kept among U.S. service records of the War of 1812 (1812–15). You may recall the tragic scene of Dudley's Massacre we visited in the chapter on Fort Meigs. (If not, turn back to read that section.)

Although Dudley's mounted battalion was referred to as Kentucky Volunteers, it was composed of men from all over the South. Dudley was a Virginian. Syms's ghost claimed to have come from Georgia. A man by the same name is listed as a private on induction into the unit and when discharged from it. He was one of the lucky few who survived the slaughter endured by his fellow troops. So many of his comrades met their end when ambushed by Native forces in the thick woods outside Fort Meigs. On the cusp of victory against the British, most of Dudley's men fell for the trap laid by Tecumseh's warriors.

Did James Syms survive Dudley's Massacre only to be murdered in this famous house twenty-eight years later?

And then we have the matter of one John Cleves, the villain. For a time, this man owned Woodbury House. As the story goes, he rented a room to a poor unsuspecting, elderly Syms. Once his guest was sound asleep, Cleves took to the defenseless man with an axe, defiled his body by removing the head and then sold what few possessions Syms had. No one suspected the murder, as no locals knew the traveling salesman. Had this been a perfect crime?

And what are we to make of Major Ward's repeated claim that John Cleves was convicted of having an incestuous relationship with his sister, a crime for which he spent time in the Ohio Penitentiary? This salacious assertion is made with such specificity that it bears further investigation. With the help of the archival library of the Ohio History Connection, the prison record of one John Cleves was indeed discovered. Born to a farmer in Pennsylvania, Cleves was convicted of the crime of incest in a court in Wood County in 1851. At forty years old, he was sentenced to five years in the infamous penitentiary. He began his sentence on July 3 of that year (inmate no. 2400) and was discharged at the end of his sentence on June 27, 1856.

Booking records have him listed on arrival as five feet, five and eleven-sixteenths inches tall, with "nearly black hair and newly sunburnt complexion." He had a medium-high, narrow forehead, with visible scars on the left side of his chin and above his right eye. His habits were listed as "temperate." Under the column "Residence of Relatives" is included the ominous phrase, "has sister in Wood Co." Property owned by Cleves on incarceration included eight head of cattle. Other notes included his being able to read and write but being "slow of speech."

One final piece of evidence, one that ties a few elements together, comes from the 1860 U.S. Federal Census. Dwelling number 318 of Plain Township, Wood County, Ohio, was owned by a forty-five-year-old English farmer named Robert Bradbrook. He lived with his wife, three children, a "trader" named John McCrory and a forty-seven-year-old laborer named John Cleves.

In Summary

The glory of the pioneer's mansion once known as Woodbury House soon evolved into something menacing and feared. Despite this, people marched long distances through a dreadful swamp just to see it. We know this was true even before the place developed a haunted reputation. It's that undying sense of wonder about the world that drives so many of us. Perhaps it's what drove you to purchase this book.

The land on which we tread, be it in Northwest Ohio or elsewhere, has witnessed countless events through the ages. Most occurrences are mundane. Others, like the claims made in this ancient bit of folklore, assert that the echoes of dastardly acts linger on in some places. Perhaps those of us who die terrible deaths remain stuck in this world, harassing the living and demanding justice.

Historical records suggest that men named McCrory, Syms and Cleves all once existed in this area of Wood County and at this exact time.

And yet...

Major Ward couldn't have known that nearly a century and a half later, his story would once more be shared and read by Wood County residents. He certainly didn't know that many of his details would prove true in a world where records are easily found with a few keystrokes.

We are left to wonder at it all, which is not a bad way to end up most days. Let's keep wondering.

BIBLIOGRAPHY

1. Man-in-Tan: BGSU's Forgotten Ghost

Periodical Articles

Bee Gee News, September 25, 1940, 1, 4; October 9, 1940, 1, 2; November 13, 1940, 1, 2; November 20, 1940, 1, 2; December 4, 1940, 1, 2, 4; January 15, 1941, 1; February 5, 1941, 1, 2; February 12, 1941, 1; February 26, 1941, 1, 2, 4; March 5, 1941, 1, 2, 4; March 19, 1941, 1, 4; May 7, 1941, 1, 2; May 14, 1941, 2, 4; September 6, 1941, 2; September 24, 1941, 2, 4; March 14, 1945, 1; October 23, 2008, 3.

News-Messenger (Fremont, Ohio), March 16, 1945, 12.

Sandusky (OH) Register, January 24, 1942, 6; March 4, 1942, 10; March 11, 1942, 7; May 6, 1942, 8; January 21, 1943, 12; April 10, 1943, 1, 8; June 30, 1943, 6; November 16, 1943, 2; April 6, 1944, 2; June 22, 1944, 1; July 20, 1944, 1; March 10, 1945, 1; March 15, 1945, 1, 8; March 28, 1945, 1; November 12, 1945, 1; May 29, 2019.

Government and Other Records

Arriving Passenger and Crew Lists (including Castle Garden and Ellis Island), 1820–1957.

Bowling Green State University yearbooks, 1940–43.

Headstone and Interment Records for U.S., Military Cemeteries on Foreign Soil, 1942–49.

U.S. Census Records, 1930, 1940.

World War II Army Enlistment Records, 1938–46.

World War II Draft Cards Young Men, 1940–47.

World War II Hospital Admission Card Files, 1942–54.

Websites

American War Memorials Overseas. "Berardi, Nello (Lconcllo) L. www.uswarmemorials. org.

BG Falcon Media. "Creepy Campus Encounters." October 31, 2006. https://www. bgfalconmedia.com.

Bowling Green State University. "Fallen Heroes." www.bgsu.edu.

———. "Recwell Rewind: First Gymnasium Constructed in 1915." March 7, 2016. https://blogs.bgsu.edu.

Fields of Honor Database. "Berardi, Robert M." www.fieldsofhonor-database.com.

Find a Grave. "PVT Nello Leo Berardi." www.findagrave.com.

———. "SGT Robert Marino Berardi." www.findagrave.com.

Honor States. "Robert M. Berardi." www.honorstates.org.

U.S. Army Center of Military History. "102nd Infantry Division." https://history.army.mil.

Wikipedia. "Netherlands American Cemetery." https://en.wikipedia.org.

———. "102nd Infantry Division (United States)." https://en.wikipedia.org.

———. "Operation Grenade." https://en.wikipedia.org.

2. FOR EDMUND KEEP(S)

Periodical Articles

Akron Beacon Journal, January 12, 1924, 15; December 23, 1926, 26.

Cincinnati Commercial Tribune, December 24, 1926, 3.

Cincinnati Enquirer, December 2, 1923, 32; December 4, 1923, 11.

Cincinnati Post, February 29, 1924, 18.

Daily News-Tribune (Oberline, OH), December 5, 1923, 3.

Daily Sentinel Tribune (Bowling Green, OH), February 18, 1918, 1, columns 1, 2; February 19, 1918, 1, columns 1, 2; February 21, 1918, 2, column 7; January 8, 1923, 1, column 6, 3, column 6; December 3, 1923, 1, column 1, 2; 4, column 4; December 23, 1926, 1, column 2.

Dayton (OH) Daily News, March 3, 1924, 1.

Evening Independent (Massillon, OH), December 4, 1923, 9; January 10, 1924, 10.

Hamilton (OH) Daily News, May 13, 1922, 7.

Journal News (Hamilton, OH), January 19, 1924, 1.

Lancaster (OH) Eagle-Gazette, January 11, 1924, 1.

Lima (OH) Gazette & The Lima Republican, December 2, 1923, 1; December 4, 1923, 1, 8; January 10, 1924, 2.

Lima (OH) News, December 3, 1923, 4; January 11, 1924, 7.

News-Herald (Cleveland, OH), December 4, 1923, 3; April 3, 1924, 9.

News-Journal (Mansfield, OH), December 2, 1923, 2.

News-Messenger (Fremont, OH), February 2, 1924, 1; January 12, 1924, 2.

Perrysburg (OH) Journal, June 21, 1890, 4; June 28, 1890, 5; February 21, 1918, 1.

Pittsburg (PA) Post-Gazette, December 2, 1923, 4; December 6, 1923, 11.

Pittsburg (PA) Press, December 2, 1923, 10.
Record-Argus (Greenville, PA), December 1, 1923, 1.
Sandusky (OH) Register, December 2, 1923, 1.
Sandusky (OH) Star Journal, December 1, 1923, 14; March 1, 1924, 2.
Times Recorder (Zanesville, OH), January 19, 1924, 1.
Wood County (OH) Sentinel, December 6, 1923, 1, column 1.
Xenia (OH) Evening Gazette, December 23, 1926, 1.

Websites

Find a Grave. "Edmund Ethelbert Keep." www.findagrave.com.
———. "Frank W. Simonds." www.findagrave.com.

Archival Resources

Official Roster of Ohio Soldiers, Sailors, and Marines in the World War, 1917–18. Columbus, OH: F.J. Heer Printing Co., 1926.
Ohio, U.S., Soldier Grave Registrations, 1804–1958.
U.S. Army Transport Service Arriving and Departing Passenger Lists, 1910–39.
U.S. Census Records, 1850, 1860, 1870, 1890, 1900, 1910, 1920.
U.S. World War I Draft Registration Cards, 1917–18.

3. Fort Meigs: Spirits of the War of 1812

Books

Lorrain, Alfred M. *The Helm, The Sword and The Cross: A Life Narrative*. Cincinnati, OH: Poe & Hitchcock, 1862.
Lossing, Benson, J. *Pictorial Field-Book of the War of 1812*. Kessinger Publishing, 1869.

Periodical Articles

Crestline (OH) Advocate, October 11, 2000, 10.
Delphos (OH) Herald, October 19, 2012, 18.
News-Messenger (Fremont, OH), May 10, 1979, 7.
Perrysburg (OH) Journal, June 4, 1886, 2.
Sandusky (OH) Register, October 24, 2007, 30.
Springfield (OH) News-Sun, October 12, 2016, B3.

Websites

Dray, April. "The Story behind This Haunted Battlefield in Ohio Is Truly Creepy." Only In Your State. https://www.onlyinyourstate.com.

Fort Meigs. https://fortmeigs.org.
Old Northwest Military Association. https://onmha.org.
Stephens, Steve. "Travel: A Visit to Fort Meigs in Perrysburg Offers History and Garrison Ghost Walks." *Columbus (OH) Dispatch*, October 3, 2021.
Wikipedia. "Fort Meigs." en.wikipedia.org.
———. "Siege of Fort Meigs." en.wikipedia.org.

4. THE LEGEND OF HOLCOMB ROAD

Periodical Articles

News-Messenger (Fremont, OH), October 27, 1975, 7.
Sentinel-Tribune (Bowling Green), October 11, 2018.

Websites

BG Falcon Media. "Ghost Stories: Creepy Legends of Wood County." November 4, 2021. https://www.bgfalconmedia.com.
Fringe Paranormal. "Holcomb Woods." June 28, 2018. https://fringeparanormal.wordpress.com.
Ohio Exploration Society. "Holcomb Road—Contribution." www.ohioexploration.com.
———. "Wood County Hauntings and Legends." https://www.ohioexploration.com.
Visit BG Ohio. "The Legend of Holcomb Road." April 12, 2019. https://visitbgohio.org.

5. INDIAN HILLS: ROSSFORD'S NATIVE HERITAGE

Periodical Articles

Circleville (OH) Herald, May 9, 1969, 5.
Coshocton (OH) Tribune, November 18, 1973, 4.
Findlay (OH) Republican Courier, May 23, 1961, 9.
———. May 21, 1971, 7–8.
Marion (OH) Star, August 24, 1968, 5.
News-Messenger (Fremont, OH), March 14, 1968, 20.
Piqua Daily Call (Troy, OH), August 22, 1968, 6.
Sentinel-Tribune (Bowing Green, OH), February 9, 2022; April 6, 2022; June 9, 2022.
Van Wert (OH) Times Bulletin, August 31, 1968, 21; August 26, 1975, 7.

Academic Resources

Stothers, David M. "Indian Hills (33W04): A Protohistoric Assistaeronon Village in the Maumee. River Valley of Northwestern Ohio." *Ontario Archaeology* 36 (1981): 47–56.

Tucker, Patrick Martin. "A Stylistic Analysis of a Protohistoric Ceramic Assemblage from Indian Hills (33-WO-4) Rossford, Ohio." Master's thesis, University of Toledo, 1981.

Websites

Advisory Council on Historic Preservation. "An Introduction to Section 106." https://www.achp.gov.

Brewer, Graham Lee. "Search for Native Missing Artifacts Led to the Discovery of Bodies Stored in the 'Most Inhumane Way Possible.'" NBC News, September 4, 2022 https://www.nbcnews.com.

Brewer, Graham Lee, and Mary Hudetz. "Senators Press for Faster Repatriation of Native American Remains." NBC News, April 21, 2023. https://www.nbcnews.com.

Ohio History Connection. "About Section 106." https://www.ohiohistory.org.

———. "American Indian Policy Supplement." March 18, 2021. https://www.ohiohistory.org.

———. "The Repatriation Database." April 26, 2023. https://projects.propublica.org.

Rossford Information and Trainspotting." Facebook. https://www.facebook.com.

Sandlin, Michael. "They Don't Want to Go in and Disturb Something They Shouldn't Disturb." WTOL Newscast, April 21, 2022. https://www.wtol.com.

U.S. General Services Administration. "Section 106: National Historic Preservation Act of 1966." https://www.gsa.gov.

WBGU-PBS. "News Six Archives. Indian Hills Elementary 1998" (video, 10:07). YouTube, April 27, 2020. https://www.youtube.com/watch?v=zJve0qYoLUQ.

6. HAUNTED SOUTH MAIN SCHOOL

Periodical Articles

Daily Sentinel Tribune (Pomeroy, OH), July 24, 1908, 3, column 6; July 25, 1908, 1, column 3; July 27, 1908, 1, column 4; July 29, 1908, 1, columns 1, 2.

Logan County (OH) News, July 24, 1908, 8.

Perrysburg (OH) Journal, July 31, 1908, 1.

Wood County (OH) Free Press, March 30, 1909, 1, column 5.

Wood County Sentinel (Bowling Green, OH), July 30, 1908, 5, column 5; July 30, 1908, 1, column 7.

Websites

Fringe Paranormal. https://fringeparanormal.wordpress.com.

Haunted South Main School. https://hauntedsouthmainschool.wordpress.com.

7. A Tale of Tontogany

Periodical Articles

Akron (OH) Daily Democrat, July 17, 1895, 1.

Chicago Tribune, March 9, 1895, 5; July 11, 1895, 7.

Chillicothe (OH) Gazette, July 17, 1895, 3.

Cincinnati Commercial Gazette, May 2, 1895, 1.

Cincinnati Enquirer, July 9, 1895, 9.

Defiance (OH) Evening News, July 12, 1895, 1.

Democratic Northwest and Henry County News (Napoleon, OH), July 11, 1895, 5.

Douglas County Herald (Ava, MO), March 28, 1895, 1.

Evening Republican (Meadville, PA), July 10, 1895, 1.

News-Journal (Mansfield, OH), April 7, 1895, 1

Perrysburg (OH) Journal, March 16, 1895, 1; July 13, 1895, 1; July 20, 1895, 1.

St. Louis Post-Dispatch, July 14, 1895, 6.

Wood County Sentinel (Bowling Green, OH), March 7, 1895, 1, 3; March 14, 1895, 1; March 21, 1895, 1; March 28, 1895, 1, 2; June 6, 1895, 3; June 13, 1895, 1, 2; July 11, 1895, 1, 3; July 18, 1895, 1, 2.

Websites

Defiance County, Ohio Genealogy. "Luther Black—Bishop Post, G.A.R." March 19, 2016. http://defiancecountyohiogenealogy.blogspot.com.

Find-A-Grave. "Catherine Eddmon." www.findagrave.com.

———. "Dr. Adam Eddmon." www.findagrave.com.

———. "Henry Perry Bernthisel." www.findagrave.com.

———. "Olive J. Peaney." www.findagrave.com.

———. "Peter Peaney." www.findagrave.com.

———. "Tontogany Cemetery." www.findagrave.com.

Haunted Toledo. "Tontogany Cemetery." Facebook, January 20, 2017. www.facebook. com.

Miami County, Ohio Genealogical Researchers. "James L. Black." https:// thetroyhistoricalsociety.org.

Wikipedia. "Tontogany, Ohio." en.wikipedia.org.

Archival Resources

Commemorative Historical and Biographical Record of Wood County, Ohio: Its Past and Present. Chicago, J.H. Beers & Co, 1897.

Compiled Marriage Index, Missouri, U.S., 1766–1983.

County Marriage Records, Ohio, U.S., 1774–1993.

Directory of Deceased American Physicians, 1804–1929.

Marriage Index, St. Louis, Missouri, U.S., 1804–76.

Marriage Records, Missouri, U.S., 1805–2002.
U.S. Census Records, 1860, 1880, 1900, 1910.

8. The Legend of Woodbury House

Books

Evers, Charles, W. *Reminiscences of Pioneer Days in Wood County and the Maumee Valley.* Bowling Green, OH: A Pioneer Scrap-Book, 1909.

Periodical Articles

Cincinnati Commercial Gazette, July 13, 1889, 12.
Perrysburg (OH) Journal, July 2, 1857, 1; July 1, 1858, 1; February 26, 1868, 2; March 11, 1887, 3.

Archival Resources

Ohio Penitentiary. Register of Prisoners and Index, Volume 2, May 1849–July 1855
U.S. Census Record, 1860.

Websites

BG Falcon Media. "Ghost Stories: Creepy Legends of Wood County." November 4, 2021. https://www.bgfalconmedia.com.
Mrs. Daffodil Digresses. "Major Ward and the Skeleton: 1852." https://mrsdaffodildigresses.wordpress.com.
Salmagundi. "Two Wood County (Ohio) Ghost Stories." November 16, 2009. http://aborer1962.blogspot.com.
Wood County Museum. Facebook, February 27, 2020. https://www.facebook.com.

ABOUT THE AUTHOR

Among many roles, Melissa R. Davies is a researcher, writer and podcaster (*Ohio Folklore*). Chief among these roles is that of a wonderer. With a little effort and a bit of curiosity, she revels in unearthing strange and nearly forgotten tales from the past. Melissa is a graduate of Defiance College and Wright State University.

She is a practicing clinical psychologist. Her day job has brought about a powerful appreciation for the transformative power of storytelling. She and her husband are native to Northwest Ohio. He lovingly endures her fascination with all things spiritual. Melissa appreciates a well-planned trip to someplace new, a full-bodied cabernet shared with friends and quiet Sundays taking long strolls down wooded trails.

FREE eBOOK OFFER

Scan the QR code below, enter your e-mail address and get our original Haunted America compilation eBook delivered straight to your inbox for free.

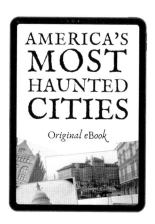

ABOUT THE BOOK

Every city, town, parish, community and school has their own paranormal history. Whether they are spirits caught in the Bardo, ancestors checking on their descendants, restless souls sending a message or simply spectral troublemakers, ghosts have been part of the human tradition from the beginning of time.

In this book, we feature a collection of stories from five of America's most haunted cities: Baltimore, Chicago, Galveston, New Orleans and Washington, D.C.